GARDENING FOR BE

WHAT TO GROW TODAY?

Basic Gardening Tips To Growing Vegetables, Hydroponics, Mini Farming, Hydropopnics, and Herb Gardening In Any Environment

AMELIE SAMPSON

Table of Contents

Introduction:

On Basic Botany and Being a Gardener

Do you have what it takes to be a gardener? Don't think too hard about this question because the answer is yes. Everyone has the capability to grow beautiful, healthy plants, no matter where they live or what type of space they have to work with. If you've got the desire to nurture, everything else can be learned. That's one of the best things about gardening- once you've got the basics figured out, you can add to your knowledge base forever.

Being a gardener is like being a scientist- you get to research plant varieties, insect species, and soil remedies until you've created the best ecosystem for your garden to thrive. You also get to be a reader and a writer- looking at seed packets and plant descriptions and keeping a journal to chronicle your garden experience. You get to be a hands-on laborer- lovingly turning your soil, tending your seedlings, and harvesting the fruits and flowers of your labor. The beauty of a garden lies not only in the things that you can grow but also in that you can grow right along with it.

- Dreaming of a garden of your own? -

Gardening can teach discipline and patience, which are lessons in humility from which we can all benefit, no matter our age or station in life. Being able to start with a tiny seed, and finish with a colorful flower or delicious tomato is a humbling, eye-opening exercise, as we watch the seed become a seedling, and blossom into a sturdy, happy plant right before our eyes. Yes, being a gardener means many things, but mostly it means that you're willing to learn, nurture, and be an active participant in creating beauty.

The Four Elements of Basic Botany

Plants are simple creatures. They need few things to survive, and when you provide those things in just the right combinations, they will thrive and return your attention with flowers and food to fill your home and your pantry with comfort and beauty. Let's take a look at those elements and the roles they play in plant health, because once you've learned the basics, you'll have a solid foundation to begin the planning stages of a garden to call your own.

Soil is the first element we'll examine because soil is not only the structural foundation of your garden, it's also the means through which your plants will receive their nutrients. For our purposes, we'll talk about soil in the traditional sense, although through hydroponics and aquaculture, it is possible to grow plants without soil as a medium. Soil is crucial for plant health because it contains the macronutrients- nitrogen, phosphorus, and potassium (N, P, K)- that plants need to perform all their basic biological functions.

Soil pH is also an important factor in soil health. Too high or too low, and your plants won't be able to properly metabolize nutrients. The optimal soil pH for most species is between 5.5. to 7.0, although there are some varieties that prefer to be in more acidic or more alkaloid soil. When you're growing a traditional garden, part of the routine is monitoring and occasionally testing the soil to make sure it's staying within pH parameters and has enough nutrients to sustain plant life. If you're planting in raised beds and containers, you'll be importing soil, and so this routine will be a little different. The other vital role of soil is to provide support for your plants to grow. You want loose, well-aerated soil that will give roots room to expand and take hold, and that will be a sponge to retain water and prevent run-off.

Water is the next element you'll need to provide for a successful garden. Water performs several important functions within your plants; it is the medium by which nutrients travel through the stem, leaves, and roots. It's also necessary for building healthy cells and cell walls, which are responsible for giving the plant structure and strength. Without water, a plant won't long survive, because water is one of the crucial components of photosynthesis, the process by which plants make their own carbohydrates for fuel.

Air is vital for plant health for a couple of reasons. The first is that plants respire, similarly to all other living things. Plants take in atmospheric gases through small openings called stomata, found on the undersides of their leaves. These gases, primarily oxygen, nitrogen, and carbon dioxide, are used to fuel the plant's biological functions. Carbon dioxide is the gas that powers photosynthesis, and oxygen is a waste product, which is then released back out of the stomata and into the atmosphere. So, yes, plants suck in CO_2 and give us back O_2- an exchange for which we should all be thankful.

The second big reason that air is so vital to plants is that proper airflow keeps your plants healthy and happy. When plants are allowed good airflow, they are less prone to pests and pathogens. Microorganisms flourish in damp environments, and if your plants don't have proper airflow, the leaves and stems will become wet and invite pests and diseases to settle in and make a home amongst your garden. Spacing your garden so your plants have room to breathe will make all the difference in dealing with pests and pathogens.

Light is the last basic factor in growing strong, healthy plants. While there are some plants that thrive with little sunlight, in general, most flower, fruit, vegetable, and herb varieties will require a minimum of 6 hours of sun each for any wildlife activity so you know what you'll be dealing with protecting your plants from. You should also get a soil test done to determine if you'll need to do any amendments before you plant. Your local Cooperative Extension or Farm Bureau will be able to help you out getting a low-cost test kit. These typically take about one to two business weeks for return results, giving you plenty of time to plan your garden while you wait.

Typically, traditional gardens are designed and built with squares and rectangles, but you don't have to stick to the norm. Designing your garden can be really fun, and all you need is some paper and pencils, a good eraser, and a straight-edge and/or compass. Measure the site you're considering, and draw it out to scale on a large piece of paper. Yes, you can also do this with one of several software applications, but there's something especially satisfying about drawing it on paper. It gives you a hands-on connection to your garden before you've even moved a shovelful of soil.

When you are choosing how to design the beds in your garden, think about what you realistically need. How much food do you want to produce? The general rule is that you need 200 sq. feet of garden space per person, assuming everyone in your family is good about eating their veggies. If you want to grow things to preserve, like cucumbers for pickles, you should consider that as well. Also, think about labor. Who will be caring for the garden? If it's only you, then plan accordingly for how much space you can maintain over the course of a growing season. There is no shame in starting small and adding to your garden in subsequent years. It's better to do that than start big, feel overwhelmed, fall behind, and either waste food, or worse, feel bad about yourself as a gardener.

You can create one big rectangle, but that's boring and can be difficult to maintain. Instead, consider squares- they are easy to work around and reach into, can be arranged in neat patterns, and can still be enclosed with one large fence to protect from wildlife. You can also consider circles, for the same reason. Be creative! You want to build a space you can enjoy for its beauty and functionality, not just its productivity. Think about other elements you can add to the design to make it a place you'll want to work and hang out. Maybe a birdbath, or a bench? How about a bistro table, so you can enjoy your morning coffee while you go about your weeding and watering routine? The possibilities are endless!

Sketch a few designs, and pin them up somewhere where you can see them regularly. I guarantee that within a few days of seeing those drawings on the refrigerator, one will become your favorite. The design you make with your head and love with your heart is always a good choice because you feel protective and nurturing of having created it. One of the greatest rewards of being a gardener is feeling proprietary of your space, knowing it's something you built with your own creativity and labor.

Once you've settled on the design you'll be using for your garden, it's time to break ground. For this step, you'll need a measuring tape, some stakes, twine, and a hammer, and whatever tool you've decided to use to break your soil. This could be hand tools, like a shovel, garden ax, and pitchfork, or a mechanical implement like a roto-tiller or small garden tractor. Your first step will be to measure and mark out your dimensions with your twine and stakes. Then double check-it so you know you're digging up the right spots! You want to till down and turn over the soil at least six to eight inches. When you are done, leave it alone for a few days to dry out and 'rest'. You should relax a bit too! Tilling is hard work, but it's fun to see your dream garden starting to take shape right before your eyes.

If you've gotten your soil test results back, your report will tell you everything you need to know about the nutrient content and pH of your soil, and if anything's not quite right, you'll be given specific instructions on how to amend it. You may find recommendations for adding lime, potash, fertilizer, or other amendments. If so, do this according to the 'dosages' on your report. If you are unsure how to do this or want to be certain you are reading the report correctly, you should contact the Farm Bureau or Cooperative Extension where you acquired your test kit and ask them to assist you. Soil amendments, even if you decide to use organic solutions, are nothing to mess around with. There can be too much of a good thing, and you don't want to cause toxicity in your garden soil.

Even if you don't have any recommended soil amendments, it's a good idea to prep your soil before planting with some compost to add organic matter. Healthy soil is a living, breathing entity, packed with microorganisms and insect life. When you add organic matter to your garden, you are providing nutrition to the underground ecosystem that will greatly benefit your plants. These organisms excrete nitrogen that plants need to thrive and enrich your soil structure by increasing pore space. This allows more room for roots to expand and lets the soil retain more water. You can never- let me emphasize- *never* have too much organic matter in your garden soil.

If you can get compost in bulk, that's awesome, but if you can't, bagged compost works well, too. You should also invest in a bag of good organic fertilizer granules. Now that your freshly-turned soil has had a few days to sit and rest, it will be drier and easier to turn in the compost and fertilizer. According to the package directions, sprinkle the appropriate amount of fertilizer granules for the size of your garden, and then spread an even layer of compost over the soil. Using a pitchfork, turn the compost, fertilizer, and soil over once or twice. You don't have to go crazy, just start incorporating everything. When you've finished, water the empty garden. You want to give the whole thing a good soaking to start leeching the compost and fertilizer down into the soil.

Now that you've got your plot turned and prepared, it's time to start thinking about what plants you want to grow and what supplies you'll need to begin and maintain your garden. Below, you will find a list of the basics you might want for seeding, planting, and maintenance, some of which we already discussed in the design and tilling phase:

- seedling cells, trays, or small containers

- potting soil

- trowel

- hand rake

- weeding fork

- sturdy gardening gloves

- foam kneeler or stool

- hand pruners

- utility scissors/utility knife

- shovel/spade

- hoe/garden ax

- pitchfork

- garden rake/leaf rake

- watering can/hose

- weed bucket/basket

- trellises/stakes/veggie cages

- twine

- garden cart or wheelbarrow

- a storage bucket, chest, or shed to keep your tools safe and dry

- metal fence posts and a roll of chicken wire or snow fencing

- a notebook or journal, or software viable for journaling

There are a lot of fancy gardening gadgets available on the market, like with any hobby, but you don't need to go all out on tools. Look for bargains and end-of-season sales, and search listings on your local online buy/sell/trade groups. Even tools that have seen better days can be fixed up quickly with a good sharpening, or sanding and painting of the handle. You can keep your budget down by being a secondhand shopper and trying not to fall prey to Shiny New Tool Syndrome.

Once you've outfitted yourself with the supplies you need and want, it's time to move on to the fun part (yes, I know I keep saying every part is the fun part!), and that's choosing seeds and seedlings to populate your garden. It's also time to crack open your garden journal. Make a note of the dimensions of your brand new garden plot, and record your dates of tillage, composting, and fertilization. You can also tuck your design sketches into the journal for future reference. Now you can begin to jot down seeds and seedlings that interest you so you can look whether those varieties will be right for your garden.

Chapter 2: Choosing Seeds and Plants for Beginners and Novices

Before you get your heart set on certain plants, the first thing you need to know is your plant hardiness zone. This is the climate region in which you reside, and in the United States, they are assigned and monitored by the Department of Agriculture. When you're choosing seeds and seedlings, you're going to want to choose varieties that are indicated to grow well in your hardiness zone.

For vegetable gardening, this isn't as restrictive as it is for ornamental plants; those tend to be a little pickier about their growing conditions. The main consideration about growing zones and vegetables is the length of the growing season in your region, and being sure to choose varieties that will have enough time to grow, flower, fruit, and be harvested if you live in a zone with a short season. In warmer zones, you may be able to get two full sowings and harvests complete in one growing season. For our purposes, we're going to split the difference and use examples and information that applies to growing vegetables in a temperate zone.

So now that you know that you're going to be looking for your hardiness zone on seed packets and seedlings, what other information can we find on those tags or catalog listings? There's actually a ton of pertinent data to be found, so let's go over what you'll find:

- Seed packets will tell you EVERYTHING you need to know for a full growing season -

- Species and variety, often both the scientific and common name

    - This will help you know if you've got the correct seeds or seedlings, based on what you've decided to grow. It's also a fun exercise to learn both names, you can whip out the Latin at dinner parties and impress your friends.

- Photo and description of the mature plant, including size

    - This will give you an idea of what you can expect when the plant is full-grown, given that it develops properly. Some seed packets will indicate whether the variety is good for containers, as well. This generally means that the plant is compact, which means it will work in small garden spaces, too.

- Mature qualities of the flowers, fruit, veggies, or herbs

- By knowing what the 'finished product' will look like, you'll know what to expect as the plant is growing and will be able to judge if it's progressing correctly. And because humans eat with their eyes, it's nice to see ripe fruits and veggies so we can choose to grow what's most appealing to us to eat.

- Hardiness zone

- We've already discussed how important this is, but just to reiterate, you want to make sure you're putting the right plants into your garden. You'll have happier plants and a happier, less frustrated you.

- Sowing, transplanting, and plant spacing guidelines

- Knowing whether your seeds need to be planted indoors or directly into the garden is a valuable piece of information. You'll also need to know seed depth and spacing, and when to plant and transplant- so be sure to read this part of the packet carefully, and either write the info in your garden journal or save the packet.

- Watering requirements

- As a general rule, native soil vegetable gardens need approximately four inches of water a week to thrive. Seed and plant descriptions found on the packaging will tell you if plants require extra or less water for optimal growth. To be honest, you'll most often see phrasing like 'keep soil evenly moist'. The best way to do this is to just water every day unless you've had or are expecting a good soaking rain.

- Sun requirements

- Vegetables are sunseekers, and most packets will tell you that the plants require full sun. Some herbs, fruit, flowers, and other ornamentals may tolerate partial or full shade, but for the purposes of a traditional vegetable garden, expect to see 'full sun' on the packets. This is a minimum of six hours a day.

- Days to germinate and days to maturity/harvest

- This information tells you how long it will take for your plant to emerge from the seed, and then grow, mature, and bear harvestable fruit. Some varieties will produce one crop and be done, and some will continue to bear fruit until for the rest of the season. Knowing when to expect your first harvest lets you decide what varieties you'd like to plant, helps you track the progress of your vegetables as they grow, and gives you a guideline about when you can begin harvesting.

- Whether the seeds are heirloom/hybrid/GMO or non-GMO

- Here's another little botany lesson, and what you ultimately decide to plant is based on personal preference. Plants that are 'heirloom' are genetic copies of their parent plant, cultivated from the seeds that those plants produce. If you save a seed from an heirloom variety, you can sow it and get the same exact plant. 'Hybrid' varieties have been carefully crossbred by botanists or agriculturalists to exhibit the desirable traits of two or more heirloom varieties. The seeds of hybrid plants can be planted, but there is no guarantee that you will get the same plant. You may get a plant that exhibits the traits of one of its parent varieties.

- That brings us to the GMO/non-GMO discussion. GMO stands for 'genetically modified organism', which immediately turns some people off, because who wants to eat mutant food? GMOs were originally created to fill a need that hybrids and heirlooms cannot, and one of the first successful agricultural applications was to create a variety of corn that could grow in arid conditions, therefore being able to create a larger food supply in destitute African desert nations. The first commercially available GMO food in the United States was the Flavr Savr tomato, which you might remember if you're of a certain age. It was genetically modified to delay ripening off the vine, so it stayed fresher longer on supermarket shelves. Today, GMOs get a bad rap not because of the science, but because of their applications and the questionable motives of some of the companies that produce them. Whether you choose GMO or non-GMO seeds and plants is entirely up to you, but at least you're now armed with the background to make that choice or do more research, should you choose.

- *Name of the producer or seed company with contact information*

- On seed packets and plant tags, you will see the name of the company, an address, and more often than not these days, a website or social media icon. In the United States, the USDA requires that producers provide this contact information, and many other countries similarly regulate their agricultural products. One great thing to benefit gardening hobbyists in the internet era is instant customer service and reliable online product information. You can hop on your computer, find the seed company's website and either find the answer to your questions or speak directly with someone who can. It's a blessing to beginning gardeners to have a direct route to speak with the company that produced their garden seeds.

- *The 'Best by' date*

    - This is the company's date of viability, and it's usually two to three years. While many seeds, if stored properly, will be viable for much longer, seed companies want you to use them by the date stamped for best results. If you've got some old seeds laying around and you're not sure if they're still good, take a couple, place them in a damp paper towel for a couple of days, and see if they begin to open up and germinate. If they do, seeds are still good. If not, toss them in the compost heap. Sometimes instead of a date, the packet will say 'packed for 20xx growing season' or something similar. That still lets you know how old the seeds are.

- *The quantity*

    - Seeds, like people, come in all shapes and sizes. You may have two packets of seeds that are the same exact dimensions, but open them up, and you'll find several hundred carrot seeds in one and two dozen pumpkin seeds in the other. The most common measurements for seed quantities in a packet are the number of seeds, by the ounce, or by the gram. Pay attention to this, especially if you're purchasing seeds online. Miss a unit of measurement, and you may be keeping your entire neighborhood in tomatoes for the next twenty years.

As you can see, seed packets, plant tags, and catalog listings can pack a lot of information into a small space, but that's great! These tags give you everything you need to know about that specific plant. There aren't too many other products on the market today aside from a seed packet that can give the consumer that much information in such a small space.

There can be so many varieties to choose from that it's easy for beginning gardeners to get overwhelmed. Let's take a look at some common kitchen garden items that are easy to grow and maintain, and will give you a great harvest from year one.

- Tomatoes

- You'd be hard-pressed to find anyone who doesn't like tomatoes in some shape or form- even if it's just in ketchup. There is a tomato variety out there for everyone, from classic beefsteaks to the tiniest cherry tomato. Tomatoes are a classic summer fruit (yes, fruit!) of the nightshade family. Tomato seeds should be started indoors and transplanted to the garden once the threat of frost has passed. When given enough water and sunlight, tomato plants will grow strong and healthy, but require stakes or caging because the weight of the fruit can cause the plants to sag and tip over. Once a plant begins to fruit, it will bear harvest until late in the season. Even the end of the year's green tomatoes can be taken in and used to make fried green tomatoes and salsa verde. Tomato plants are very heavy feeders and may require fertilization during the growing season to stay on track.

- Beans/peas

- Beans and peas, which come in many varieties, are the givers of the kitchen garden. They belong to a family of leguminous plants, and legumes have a really cool function- they can put nitrogen back into the soil as they grow! This is due to a symbiotic relationship formed with a soil microorganism known as rhizobia. The roots of the legumes exude excess sugar from photosynthesis, which the rhizobia latch onto in droves. Their nitrogen waste replenishes the soil around the roots of the legumes. Beans and peas come in both bush and vining varieties, require regular water and light, and grow quickly when sown directly in the garden in early spring. Harvest them early and often for a continuous flow of fresh beans and peas, which can be eaten raw or cooked, or dried, frozen, and canned to preserve them for the off-season. Vining varieties should be trellised or staked to provide support for climbing.

- Cucumbers

- Cucumbers belong to the cucurbit family, and they also come in a lot of neat varieties. The classic cucumber is a long, dark green fruit, but smaller varieties and color variations are common these days. The cucumber hasn't changed much over the centuries- Roman records show that cucumbers were grown for the ruling class during the height of the empire, and seem to indicate that the plant originated in the region of what's now modern Armenia. Cucumbers aren't fussy plants and can be grown in small spaces in bush varieties. Vining varieties can be trellised to grow in small spaces or protect the plants from mildew from laying on the damp ground. Cucumbers will continue to produce as long as they are harvested, so be prepared to eat a lot of salad and make a lot of pickles if you grow a lot of cucumber plants.

- Peppers

- Peppers also belong to the nightshade family, and you don't have a be a fan of spicy food to grow and enjoy peppers. There are plenty of sweet varieties, the classic bell pepper of course, plus many others. Jalapenos, poblanos, and banana peppers are also fun and easy to grow. Like their cousins the tomatoes, peppers also succeed best when sown indoors and transplanted after the last frost. Cool fact about peppers- the rainbow of colors is not indicative of different varieties! Those come from when you harvest the fruit. A pepper is technically ripe when it is of size and becomes a shiny green, but as you leave it on the vine, it will begin to change color from green, to yellow, to orange, to red. Peppers can be eaten fresh raw or cooked, or prepped and frozen for the off-season.

- Lettuces/greens

- Looseleaf lettuce and salad greens are a great place to start growing your own leafy vegetables, and they can be among the easiest and the most frustrating to grow- but the challenge is definitely worth it! The great thing about greens like lettuce, kale, and spinach is that they are cold-hardy, which means you can plant them outdoors early and enjoy them all season long. The challenge in growing greens comes from keeping woodland creatures like chipmunks, squirrels, and groundhogs away from them while they grow. Consider making little screens or putting netting over your budding greens to keep them safe while they are maturing. You don't want your tender young plants to become a rodent buffet.

- Squash

- Once you become a gardener, you'll get in on the joke about not being able to give away mid-summer zucchini. Squashes are also in the cucurbit family and they can be prolific producers. They're also heavy feeders that can rapidly deplete your garden soil, so they should be planted sparingly. One or two plants of each variety will provide you with plenty of squash for the whole season. Aside from the ubiquitous zucchini, you can plant other summer varieties, like the classic yellow, or try your hand at winter varieties like butternut, acorn, or spaghetti squash. Squash does best when sown directly into the garden after the last frost.

- Herbs

- A kitchen garden isn't complete without some herbs to cook with your fresh vegetables. Many common herbs are perennial, which means you can plant them and enjoy them for years to come. They also make great companion plants for warding off unwanted insect pests from invading your vegetable plants. Consider planting your own basil, dill, thyme, sage, rosemary, oregano, or mint- you can pick and choose based on what you like to cook. When you can step outside and snip off your own fresh herbs for dinner or dry bunches of herbs to enjoy in your winter soups and stews, it's a next-level experience for your taste buds. Many herbs can be grown from seed, starting them indoors or outdoors depending on your frost conditions.

- Alliums

- The most commonly-grown home garden alliums are onions and garlic, and since those are staples for many common recipes, wouldn't it be nice to cultivate your own? You should plan ahead to plant onions and garlic, as they are generally planted in the fall and harvested the following spring and summer. Alliums aren't usually sown from seen in a kitchen garden, but instead are grown from cuts or 'sets' from the previous year's harvest. If you decide to grow alliums, you can check out the different varieties and their characteristics by doing a little research in the summer, then choosing, purchasing, and planting your sets in the fall.

- Strawberries

- Nothing says summer like fresh berries, and strawberry plants make awesome companions for vegetables in your garden by providing ground cover and drawing pollinating insects. You can even trellis strawberry vines to grow up and around the rest of your garden, so they don't take up too much space. Strawberries are best grown from commercially-available seedlings, but once you've established them in your garden, you'll be able to enjoy them for several years.

- Melons

  - Melons are the most popular fruit in the cucurbit family because they are fabulous for summer eating and don't require much maintenance to grow. Common melon varieties are watermelon, cantaloupe, and honeydew, and there are small versions available if you don't want the vines taking over the whole garden. Most melon species should be planted outdoors in the mid-spring. They are not as heavy of feeders as their cousins the squash and cucumber, but they can be thirsty- melons have extremely high water content and require a lot of water to develop properly.

These are just some of the wide variety of plants you can grow in a traditional vegetable garden, but these are among the best 'starter' species. Once you've become more confident in your abilities, you can start to branch out into species like brassicas like broccoli and cauliflower, tubers like potatoes, and root vegetables like beets and carrots.

Chapter 3: Planting and Maintenance

Whether you decide to start your garden from seed or from nursery stock seedlings, once you've chosen what to grow, it's time to get planting. If you're going to be starting from seed, indoor or outdoor, you'll need to pay close attention to the sowing instructions on your seed packets. The spacing and depth guidelines will help you get your seeds off to the best possible start.

Sowing and Transplanting

For indoor sowing, make sure that you've got a good light source for your seedlings when they begin to sprout. If you don't have a viable window that you can set your pots or seedling cells near, you can invest in an inexpensive grow light. While some units can run on the pricier side, there are small portable units to be found for less than $50, and they can prove invaluable in your gardening endeavors. You want your newly germinated plants to get off to the best start with enough warmth, light, and water.

When it's time to transplant your seedlings, either those you've grown or those you've purchased, you also need to follow the spacing guidelines. You can use a trowel to make holes slightly deeper and wider than the seedling pots. To remove your seedlings, gently squeeze the pots to loosen the soil, and grasp the seedling by the base of the stem- never by the leaves. Settle your seedling into its new home and gently but firmly tamp the soil around the plant. Once you've got all your seedlings installed, give them a good drink, and leave them be to nestle into their spot. The last thing to do after you're all planted is to pound your fence posts into the ground and wrap your chicken wire or snow fence protection around the garden. If that's not your style, you can certainly choose to put up something more aesthetically pleasing. Be sure to mark all your planting and transplanting dates in your garden journal.

If you're unsure how to arrange the plants in your garden, it's a good rule to keep your heavy feeders apart from each other, as well as plants from the same family. You can organize your varieties by placing a legume in between your heavy feeders like peppers, tomatoes, and squash. Intermix your herbs and lighter-feeding cucurbits, and you'll have a give-and-take relationship among your plants and your soil that will avoid depleting your soil of nutrients too quickly.

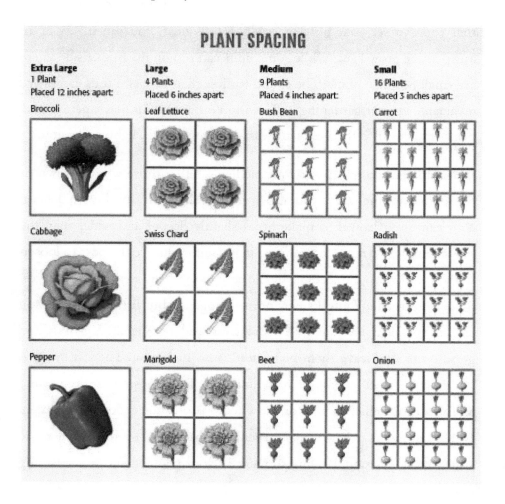

PLANT SPACING

Extra Large
1 Plant
Placed 12 inches apart:
Broccoli

Cabbage

Pepper

Large
4 Plants
Placed 6 inches apart:
Leaf Lettuce

Swiss Chard

Marigold

Medium
9 Plants
Placed 4 inches apart:
Bush Bean

Spinach

Beet

Small
16 Plants
Placed 3 inches apart:
Carrot

Radish

Onion

- Keep plant size in mind when you are planning and planting, and use recommended guidelines -

Watering

You should make a point to water your garden every day unless of course, you are expecting heavy rain. Tomatoes are a great non-scientific measure of whether or not you are overwatering- the fruit will begin to split if the tomato plants are overhydrated. Dial it back a little bit with the watering. Remember, you can always water again, but you can't mop up excess moisture if you've overwatered. If you like, you can easily install a self-watering system like drip irrigation or soaker hoses; these come in fairly inexpensive DIY kits at most garden centers or home improvement stores. Add a timer to your hose spigot, and you've got a set-it-and-forget-it watering method.

Some people love to water, whether by hose or watering can, and that's great, too. One important thing to remember when your watering your garden is to water the roots, not the leaves. Leaves aren't the part of the plant that takes in water, and wet leaves can make your plants susceptible to sunscald and pathogens. If you can, always try to water in the morning so the soil has time to dry over the course of the day. You should also avoid using sprinklers for vegetable gardens because they water unevenly and cannot target the roots. Save sprinklers for the front lawn and for the kids and grandkids to run through.

Fertilizing and Composting

Fertilizer and compost can help you get your vegetable garden through a long growing season without stripping all the nutrients from your soil.

Remember what we talked about earlier, though. Fertilizer can be toxic to your plants in too-large doses because more is not always better. Plants can suffer from nitrogen, phosphorus, and potassium toxicity just as easily as they can suffer from a deficiency. The best time to fertilize your garden is at the halfway mark of the growing season. You can use the same granulated fertilizer you used to prepare your soil for planting. Following package directions, sprinkle an appropriate amount in the garden before your morning watering. When you fertilize mid-season, it's called 'side-dressing' your plants.

Compost is always welcome. As noted before, you cannot put too much organic matter into your soil. If you have the space to start your own compost heap, that's even better, but if not, bagged or bulk will always be preferable to nothing. You don't need much space to make compost for yourself, and pallet piles are all the rage. All you need is 8 metal fenceposts, four pallets, and your pitchfork. Arrange the fenceposts in a square, so that the pallets will all slide down over the posts to create the walls. Then put all your plant waste, grass clippings, household foods scraps (no fats or meats), eggshells, used paper towels, shredded newspapers, etc. inside the square. Wet it down with the hose and cover it with a tarp- bonus points for bungee-cording it to the pallets. You can remove one pallet to use your pitchfork to turn the pile once a week or so. The material on the bottom of the pile will begin to decompose. Just keep the pile warm, wet, and turned, and you will have your own rich, crumbly compost (known as humus) to enrich your garden in no time.

This diagram is an example of the different layers. Alternating kitchen and garden waste layers with an occasional layer of manure works well.

LAYER OF HESSIAN TO RETAIN HEAT AND MOISTURE	
LOW NITROGEN	STRAW AND WATER
HIGH NITROGEN	KITCHEN WASTE
WATER	
LOW NITROGEN	GARDEN WASTE
HIGH NITROGEN	MANURE
LOW NITROGEN	COARSE PRUNINGS
HIGH NITROGEN	GRASS CLIPPINGS/PAPER
LOW NITROGEN	STRAW OR DRY LEAVES
HIGH NITROGEN	SOFT PRUNINGS
LOW NITROGEN	COARSE PRUNINGS
LOOSELY FORKED SOIL BASE	

- Composting is simple when you know what to include! -

Troubleshooting Weeds, Pests, and Disease

Now to the nuisance stuff- weeds, pests, and pathogens. The sad truth is, no matter how closely you follow best gardening practices, these three will find a way to crash the party. The next few paragraphs will take you through some ways to avoid, diagnose, and alleviate problems that may arise, and hopefully, you won't have to deal with too many of these issues as your build and cultivate your new garden.

Weeds are the 'easiest' problem to deal with, so let's start there. You can avoid many weed issues by mulching your vegetable garden, but we don't mean using regular wood chips as you might use in an ornamental garden. These can be hard to turn into the soil and may not break down at the end of the season, so they are ideal. Some hardwood chips can also leach tannins into your soil, which will disrupt the pH. Some of the best natural mulches for veggie gardens are straw (not hay!), grass clippings, and weed cloth, which is exactly what it sounds like- rolls of material you can cut and lay among your plants to cover the bare soil between them. Mulch has the added benefit of insulating the soil and helping it retain water.

When you manually weed, you can compost any material that hasn't yet gone to seed. Anything that has bolted should go in the trash- you don't want any of the seedy stuff headed back into the garden as compost the next year. You should avoid at all measures using any herbicides in your vegetable garden. Most commercially-available weed killers are broad-spectrum for broad-leaf plants, which means they will take down anything in their path. These chemicals cannot differentiate between a dandelion and a daffodil, and have no business being sprayed near your growing food. Instead, invest in mulch and a good weeding hoe. Your garden will be much happier for it.

Pests are an unfortunate part of garden life, too. You should become familiar with some of the most common vegetable garden pests, so you're not surprised when you see them. Tiny green aphids, globular slugs, and Japanese beetles are three of the most-seen garden nuisances because they aren't too picky about what you are growing. Some common species-specific pests you might see are squash vine borers, which adore cucurbits, and tomato hornworms, which as you can probably guess, love tomatoes.

Here's the thing about garden insects, though- some are super helpful. Ladybugs and praying mantises eat harmful insects, and bees, butterflies, and dragonflies are fantastic pollinators. If you see an insect in your garden, and you're not sure what it is, DON'T touch it. You don't know if it's something that can bite or cause skin irritation. If you can, take a photo. Look it up online, using the most specific search terms you can, i.e. "one-inch long black and silver beetle with large antennae found in the northern part of X county in Y state".

Once you've identified what's eating your garden, you can take appropriate steps to alleviate the problem. Chemical pesticides should be used sparingly in vegetable gardens, and you can opt for horticultural soaps and oils that do the trick nicely. You can also try pheromone traps, like the bags you'll often see hung to attract and trap Japanese beetles. Here's a neat tip to project whether or not you'll have a Japanese beetle problem in the summertime- watch how many corvids (crows, starlings, and/or ravens) come and eat from your lawn in the fall and spring. These birds LOVE grubs, which are the Japanese beetle larvae that were laid in the ground. Lots of corvids feasting= lots of grubs in your lawn = banner year for beetles.

Birds are a great way to manage insects in your garden, by the way. If you can, put birdhouses, feeders, and birdbaths around your property to attract the omnivorous local species that can help control the insect population in your garden. This type of holistic approach of using non-chemical and biological controls is called integrated pest management, or IPM. IPM is becoming a popular method for both home gardeners and large-scale growers to reduce the use of harsh pesticides that can permanently damage the ecosystem.

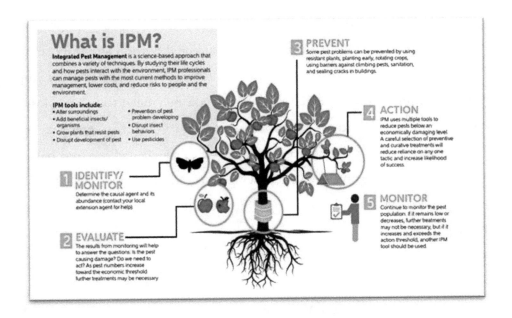

What is IPM?

Integrated Pest Management is a science-based approach that combines a variety of techniques. By studying their life cycles and how pests interact with the environment, IPM professionals can manage pests with the most current methods to improve management, lower costs, and reduce risks to people and the environment.

IPM tools include:
- Alter surroundings
- Add beneficial insects/organisms
- Grow plants that resist pests
- Disrupt development of pest
- Prevention of pest problem developing
- Disrupt insect behaviors
- Use pesticides

3 PREVENT
Some pest problems can be prevented by using resistant plants, planting early, rotating crops, using barriers against climbing pests, sanitation, and sealing cracks in buildings.

4 ACTION
IPM uses multiple tools to reduce pests below an economically damaging level. A careful selection of preventive and curative treatments will reduce reliance on any one tactic and increase likelihood of success.

1 IDENTIFY/ MONITOR
Determine the causal agent and its abundance (contact your local extension agent for help).

5 MONITOR
Continue to monitor the pest population. If it remains low or decreases, further treatments may not be necessary, but if it increases and exceeds the action threshold, another IPM tool should be used.

2 EVALUATE
The results from monitoring will help to answer the questions: Is the pest causing damage? Do we need to act? As pest numbers increase toward the economic threshold further treatments may be necessary.

- IPM can help you avoid major pest concerns in your garden -

Pathogens are another common concern for vegetable gardeners. While you can do your best to avoid creating conditions for disease to thrive, they can sometimes pop up despite your efforts. Plants can be susceptible to viruses, bacteria, fungi, and these conditions most often manifest their symptoms on the leaves of the affected plant material. Some of the most common pathogen issues in vegetable gardens are powdery and/or downy mildew, early and late blight, mosaic virus and root rot, and leaf spot or leaf curl. When you see something 'off' about your plant, you should take a photo of the affected part of the plant and do a quick online search to see what's going on.

Sometimes, you'll be able to salvage the whole plant; cucurbits are prone to powdery mildew, which makes the leaves look terrible, but doesn't affect the flowering or fruiting function of the plant. One thing you should do with all diseased plants is cut away the affected portion and dispose of it in the trash, not the compost- these aren't the good microorganisms you want in your compost heap. Other times, you may need to call it a loss, remove the plant, and move on. As long as you follow best practices by watering your roots, spacing your plants for adequate airflow, and being vigilant about identifying and removing diseased plant tissue in a timely fashion, you should be able to avoid or alleviate any pathogen issues with ease.

Chapter 4: Harvesting and Preserving

Harvesting your garden is one of the greatest joys in the whole hobby, and when's time to begin reaping what you've sown, there are a few tips you should follow. As a general rule, you should harvest in the morning before your daily watering. An old kitchen colander is one of the best harvest baskets because you can carry it inside, pop it right in the sink, and wash your morning haul. Harvesting in the morning takes the fresh fruit and veggies off the plant before the heat of the day.

You should take care to never tear the plants when you harvest. For things like beans and peas, remove the pods from the vine not at the top of the pod itself, but at the little joint where the pod's stem meets the vine. For cucurbits, try to remove the whole stem from the vine when you pick- you can do this by twisting or cutting the stem at the joint with the main stem. Tomatoes will tell you when they're ready to go by essentially falling off the vine into your hand. Bumping into a heavily-laded cherry tomato plant will send a cascade of fruit falling to the ground, and you scrambling to pick up every last juicy treasure.

You can pick some items right before they ripen, too- cucumbers and green beans are less pithy and much sweeter when picked on the small size. Smaller cukes are crunchier for making pickles, too. You should also pick squash and zucchini before they get to comical proportions, or else you'll have monsters on your hands with large, unpalatable seeds. After harvest, give your produce a good cold water rinse and pat or lay out to dry. You don't need to immediately refrigerate most fresh veggies. If anything gets bruised or split, make a point to either eat or cook and store those items the same day, or place them in the compost. Broken skin on vegetables can invite bacteria. You can make notes in your garden journal about what grew nicely and provided an abundant harvest, and what varieties didn't fare as well. It will help you make decisions about what to plant in the future.

The great thing about having a kitchen garden is having fresh produce right outside your backdoor, but you can also save your harvest for enjoyment in the off-season. The easiest way to do this is by freezing your fruits, and blanching and freezing your vegetables. Berries freeze very well, and only need a good wash before being bagged and labeled. Frozen berries can be used later for pies and smoothies, or eaten as is as a cool treat. Frozen vegetables prepared at home will outshine those you can find at the grocery store. You can freeze beans, peas, sliced peppers, sliced and shredded zucchini, and much more.

For those who are feeling more ambitious, canning is a great way to fill your pantry with pickles, jams, and salsas for the coming off-season. Most items from your garden can be canned with the simple water bath method, which requires very little equipment, and you can find cookbooks and online recipes with exceptional instructions and traditional and contemporary flavor combinations to tempt any palate. Some people like to vacuum seal their prepared foods as well, and inexpensive countertop systems have made this a great option for people who don't have much freezer space but are shy of the chore of canning.

Drying and dry storage are also among your choices for extending the life of your harvest. Beans and peas can be dried in or out of their pods and make terrific additions to soups and stews. You can also dry bunches of herbs, that can then be crumbled and stored in airtight glass or plastic jars to use for seasoning in all your favorite dishes. If you've grown onions and garlic, you can cure and store these items to enjoy for months to come! By employing any of these preservation methods, you'll be eating healthy, homegrown food long after the growing season has ended.

Chapter 5: Preparing for the Future

Once your garden has exhausted itself, it's time to think about putting it to bed for the winter. You should clean out all spent plant material and compost it, given that it is free of disease. Make sure you remove all roots, vines, and fallen fruits and vegetables, lest you accidentally seed something where it shouldn't be seeded. Spread a layer of compost in the garden and give it a quick turn. Lastly, you should put an organic ground cover on your soil- either by planting a winter cover like clover, rye, or vetch, or by spreading a layer of straw (not hay, which has seeds!). When spring comes, you can turn what left of that layer or cover crop right into the garden to improve your soil organic matter.

When you plan your garden for the following year, you should practice crop rotation to make sure that you don't put heavy feeders back into the same space which will strip the soil. Move everything one spot to the right, if you grow in rows, or one spot clockwise if you grow in squares or circles. You can do this every year so that your legumes have a chance to enrich the soil before a moderate or heavy feeder moves back in. Come spring, you'll want to turn the garden, fertilize, and compost, like you did when preparing your garden for the first time.

The off-season doesn't have to mean you stop being a gardener! Take time over the winter to browse seed catalogs, read up on new gardening gadgets, and browse online gardening resource sites. Everyone who gardens eventually finds a niche, whether it's playing around with cucumber varieties to make the best pickles, or developing herb mixes to gift to family and friends. Look for an online community of like-minded gardeners to exchange ideas with- you'll find your tribe whether you're interested in growing award-winning tomatoes or obscure bean varieties, or learning more about soil science. Take notes and jot ideas and sketches in your gardening journal, you'll be amazed at how the ideas start flowing when you start researching.

Most of all you should enjoy the journey. You've taken a bare plot of ground and turned it into a food-producing paradise, and done it in the span of just a few months! You should congratulate yourself on your success. You can now take what you've learned and become a stronger, more capable gardener with every growing season.

PART II

Urban Gardening

If you live in an urban setting, you might think that you can't be a gardener, but nothing could be further from the truth. As long as you can find some sunshine, you can be a gardener, whether you've got a balcony, a courtyard, or an entire empty lot to work with. Urban gardening can be an exercise in creativity and will reward you with food and flowers you can enjoy with family and friends, no matter how much or how little space you have. Let's start by taking a look at the special design considerations for creating a beautiful garden oasis in a concrete landscape.

Chapter 1: Planning and Building an Urban Garden

Living in a city means there often isn't a lot of open soil available for gardening unless of course, you go start tilling up a plot in a public park. Since that's likely illegal or at the very least, frowned upon, the first thing you need to do when designing an urban garden is to define your space.

If you've got a patio or balcony, then you will be able to do your gardening in containers or small growing tables. For larger spaces like courtyards, you may be able to construct small raised beds. Many residential stand-alone homes in urban areas have retaining walls built into their driveway areas, so you may be able to take advantage of these structures and carve out some terraced gardening space along these walls. Think about all the possible places that have gardening potential and observe them to see how much sun they get each day.

Another consideration for urban garden design is what's known as the heat island effect. Cities are made up of a lot of impervious surfaces like glass, concrete, asphalt, and brick. These materials collect heat during the day and release it at night, which is one of the reasons that large cities are warmer than their immediately surrounding suburbs and small towns. When you garden in a city that creates a heat island, you have to adjust to the temperatures and growing conditions that the effect creates. Because of these elevated temperatures, urban gardens require a lot of watering, so you'll need to make sure you've got a handy water source.

●How the Heat Island Phenomenon occurs

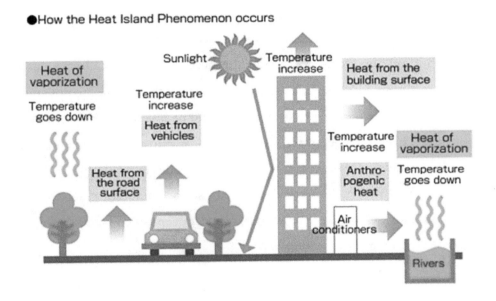

- How the urban heat island effect works -

Once you have chosen a location for your gardening endeavors, it's time to have fun designing! If you're going to be using containers, you have a lot of flexibility about what you can do. Depending on what you want to grow, you can use as few or as many containers as you'd like, given that your smallest containers are large enough to support one plant (generally eight to ten inches in diameter). You can use larger containers to group several plants together, as well.

For container plantings, height is another factor that adds dimension and interest to an urban garden. You can use small tables or homemade wooden platforms to set your pots at varying heights and make use of hanging baskets to add a top layer of depth and maximize space. You can also find commercially-made stacking and step-style planters that offer a lot of growing surface and can fit in a compact space.

If you have room to build small raised beds or install growing tables or troughs, you also need to consider the heat island effect. Placing raised beds on surfaces like asphalt and concrete means that the soil temperature in the bed will be warmer than the soil would be in a traditional native soil garden. This isn't necessarily a bad thing- it can extend your growing season and allow for succession planting, but it does mean that your garden will also be thirstier. Raised beds that are set on impervious services are most effective when they are at least two feet deep, so consider that when you are thinking about designs.

Whether you are using containers or small raised beds, you should also be mindful about placing them directly next to a building, because the building will also radiate collected heat during the night. In colder climates, this is actually a useful effect of the urban heat island, keeping tender seedlings alive during chilly evenings. In warmer climates, it can have a wilting effect on plants, who need the cooler temperatures at night to rest from extreme heat during the day.

It's recommended that no matter what type of containers, tables, or beds you decide to install, you should make them non-permanent structures, and if you are renting your home in the city, you should check with your landlord or building officials before placing any pots or raised beds. This is protective of both you and the property owner or manager. You don't want to put in a lot of effort to install things that you may be told to take down, you don't want to violate any safety or building codes, and you will also want to make sure that it's clear whether or not you intend to leave behind or take with you any gardening structures should you decide to move when your lease is up. Get everything you can in writing so there's no confusion later.

You should measure your space and sketch out your designs with pencil and paper, keeping in mind that you'll need to conserve some space around your containers or beds to have room to work. It's a lovely thought to want to cram as many plants as possible into a small area, but you want to be able to water, weed, and harvest without needing to be a contortionist. You also want to make sure your garden has good airflow. Draw a handful of designs and see which you like best, and then it's time to choose your materials.

This part of urban gardening is really fun because it can be like a scavenger hunt, both in real life and online. Try to find reclaimed materials around your city- look at rummage sales, at online buy/sell/trade and freecycle boards, and connect with the local waste authority to see if you can get discarded construction materials. You can get pots and containers that fit your tastes from quiet to quirky, and find lumber and masonry block to build your raised beds if you've got the room. If you want all your pots to match, you can also save cash by purchasing in bulk. Pre-fabricated bed kits and table kits are also an option for those who aren't inclined to DIY construction projects.

Once you've gathered your materials, you can get to assembling your garden. If you're building raised beds, make sure you've got all your tools at the ready before you begin. If you're using pre-fab kits, check to see that you've got all the parts and necessary tools on hand before you begin assembling. You don't want to get halfway through a project and realize you're short some hardware or don't have the right screwdriver. If you're cutting materials, always measure twice and cut once, as they say, to avoid goofs and waste. If you are assembling pre-fab kits, save the paperwork in case you ever need to replace any hardware, and if you've constructed your own beds, save your plans and sketches so you remember what materials you've used if you need to do any replacement or maintenance down the road.

With your raised beds built or your containers gathered, the next thing you will need is some soil. It may be difficult to get bulk soil delivered in the city, but it's worth looking into the option just in case. If you cannot, you're going to have to go with bagged soil. For containers, you can go with straight potting soil, and for raised beds, you'll want to use a 50/50 mix of potting soil and topsoil. For reference, potting soil is lighter than topsoil and contains a mineral mixture to help your plants get the necessary nutrients. Topsoil is, well, dirt, although I don't like to use that word. It's mineral and nutrient content is often inconsistent, but for filling raised beds, it will give you more bang for your buck than the expense of potting soil alone. You can always amend the soil to make it more nutrient-rich (more on that in a bit!)

The reason you want to get a good potting mix for containers is twofold. Potting soil, being lighter than topsoil, will mean that your pots won't get so heavy you shouldn't be able to move them around if necessary, although large pots can always be set on wheeled dollies if you want to be able to roll them around. The other reason is that potting soil contains nutrients to get your plants off to a good start and through much of the growing season, although heavy feeding plants may need a bit of a fertilizer nudge to avoid a mid-season slump. Look for potting soils that have sphagnum or peat moss, and vermiculite and/or perlite. Some mixes also have fertilizer built right into the product, so if you get these, you're not going to want to use additional fertilizer later, or you may risk plant toxicity.

Okay! Are you all set up? Got your garden planned, assembled, and chosen your soil? Wonderful! Now it's time to talk about plant selection and choosing the best varieties to thrive in an urban garden. You've probably got a good idea of what you would like to grow, but let's take a look at choosing seedlings and talk about some of the plants that do well in containers and small beds.

Chapter 2: Choosing Plants for Food and Fun

Many urban gardens are small, and that means that you've got to be creative about the use of space. In this section, we're going to examine what you need to know about reading plant tags to choose the best seedlings, talk about companion planting for maximizing room in your beds and containers, and go over some of the food and flower varieties that do well in limited space.

When you're planting an urban garden, it's important to look closely at plant descriptions on the tags so you know you're getting varieties that will thrive in smaller spaces. You should look for any tags that indicate 'good for containers' or 'container-friendly'. Also, look for indicators like 'compact' or 'low-growing.' Plant tags are a wealth of information and will provide you with the following data:

Hardiness zone/growing zone: This lets you know if a plant is suitable to be grown in your locale. You can find your zone on the USDA website in the United States, or your country's department of agriculture site in other locations. You can also call that department's toll-free number for assistance. This is useful if you are browsing plants in a catalog or online. Most garden centers and retail nurseries will only sell seedlings that are appropriate for your area.

Plant name, common and botanical- This will indicate the name of the plant, the variety, and the cultivar (which is a fancy way of indicating a particular color or another identifying trait). This will help you choose a variety that is appealing to you and will fit into your garden scheme.

Photos of the grown plant/produce- A picture of what you can expect when the plant is fully grown and is producing flowers and fruit is useful in knowing if your plant is growing properly. It also helps you decide if a plant is aesthetically pleasing to you.

Spacing requirements/plant dimensions- This is vital information for planting an urban garden with limited space. If you're going to be planting in raised beds, you know your dimensions and can use this data to decide how many seedlings you can fit into your garden. When you know how far apart the plants need to be and how large they will get, it's easy to avoid overbuying and overcrowding. For containers, it's useful information because it can help you decide how many plants to put in a pot, based on dimensions. Plants should be in pots of at least 8" by themselves, but you can certainly plant more seedlings together in larger containers!

Sun and water requirements- Most vegetable and herb varieties require a minimum of six to eight hours of sun per day, while ornamentals like flowers will vary. You can use this to your advantage by choosing varieties that may thrive in that one corner the sun doesn't quite reach all day or that shady spot you just couldn't avoid having as part of your garden. The watering requirements are important, too, because you don't want to over- or under-water an urban garden. We'll go over some great watering techniques in the maintenance section of this chapter.

Days to bloom -or- harvest- This tidbit lets you know how long you'll have to wait to pick your first flowers or vegetables. It also gives you a good baseline indicator that your plants are growing on track with the norm. While you may see some action before or after the length of time indicated, this is an average for the species and variety. This may also tell you if the plant is a continual harvester, how long it blooms or produces fruit, and when to know that the plant is spent, in the case of annuals.

Heirloom/hybrid/GMO or non-GMO- While this may not play much into your decision, you should be aware of the differences between these three types of plants. An heirloom variety is one that was bred from the seeds of identical plants. This means each generation of the plant has one common DNA sequence, and planting a seed from an heirloom will result in the same plant growing. A hybrid plant is one that has been cultivated from two or more strains of DNA, and the results are a plant that exhibits the best traits of the parent plants. This is often done to increase yield and disease resistance, or to produce a new color. If you save a seed from a hybrid and plant it, you may get the same plant, or you may get one that exhibits traits from its parent varieties. GMO stands for 'genetically modified organism', and you can make your own decisions about whether you want GMO or non-GMO plants, but here is some background. The original GMOs were created for commercial agriculture to increase yield, lengthen the shelf life of ripe produce, and produce drought-resistant crops that would excel in arid regions. These varieties have had their DNA altered to be able to do so.

With all this information under your belt, you can be a pro at reading and interpreting plant tags and choose the best plants to fit your budget, your space considerations, and your individual tastes. When you're planning out your plant locations, you should think heavily about companion planting, meaning that where you put your plants is just as important as which plants you choose. You can intermingle your flowers, herbs, fruits, and vegetables to be advantageous to you and to each other.

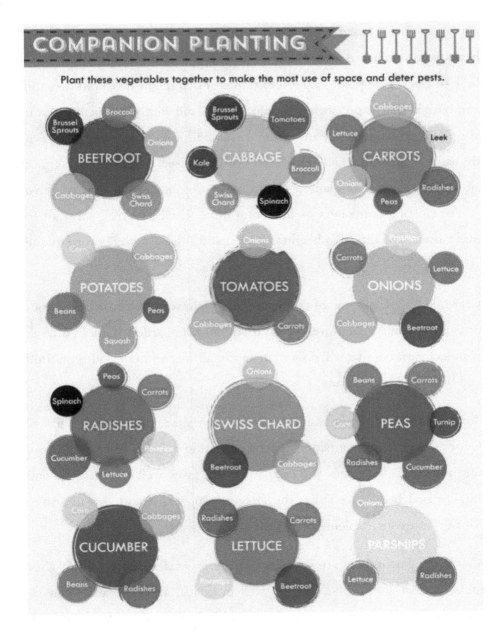

COMPANION PLANTING

Plant these vegetables together to make the most use of space and deter pests.

BEETROOT — Brussel Sprouts, Broccoli, Onions, Swiss Chard, Cabbages

CABBAGE — Brussel Sprouts, Tomatoes, Broccoli, Spinach, Swiss Chard, Kale

CARROTS — Cabbages, Leek, Radishes, Peas, Onions, Lettuce

POTATOES — Corn, Cabbages, Peas, Squash, Beans

TOMATOES — Onions, Carrots, Cabbages

ONIONS — Parsnips, Lettuce, Carrots, Beetroot, Cabbages

RADISHES — Peas, Carrots, Lettuce, Cucumber, Spinach, Parsnips

SWISS CHARD — Onions, Cabbages, Beetroot

PEAS — Beans, Carrots, Turnip, Cucumber, Radishes, Corn

CUCUMBER — Corn, Cabbages, Radishes, Beans

LETTUCE — Radishes, Carrots, Beetroot, Parsnips

PARSNIPS — Onions, Radishes, Lettuce

- A handy companion planting chart to help you maximize space -

Companion planting in an urban garden is a good way to make the most of limited growing space, repel insects, and use low-growing plants as

59

living mulch for larger varieties. In containers, it's a fun idea to add the herbs you would use in cooking or preparing the vegetables around the base of the veggie plant. A good example of this might be to put oregano and basil in a large pot with a tomato plant or dill with your cucumbers. It also helps you keep some modicum of separation between your plants of the same family or species, which can 'confuse' insect pests who may attack all similar plants. Companion planting can also be aesthetic, as in when you're creating containers of flowering ornamentals. There, you want to mix varieties of differing heights, colors, and foliage textures for striking visual appeal.

Let's take a look at some of the plants you might want to consider for your urban gardening adventure. These tried-and-true garden staples come in compact varieties that will do well in any small space and provide you food and beauty all season long.

Tomatoes- These tasty members of the nightshade family are a global favorite, and many container varieties thrive in urban gardens. You can find tomatoes of all sizes and colors that will grow well in containers and small raised beds, given that they have enough space to spread strong roots, and are given plenty of healthy soil and water.

Cucumbers- Cucumbers are another favorite in gardens everywhere. They make perfect summer snacks, go well in salads, and of course, can be pickled. This hardy member of the cucurbit family can be found in bush varieties, or you can choose vining varieties if you're interested in doing some vertical gardening (check out the upcoming segment on that!)

Beans/peas- These versatile members of the legume family are a great addition to any garden, but the wealth of compact varieties are perfect for small urban endeavors. Legumes even have a superpower! They add nitrogen, a much-needed macronutrient, back into the soil, which means planting them next to heavy feeders like tomatoes in a raised bed benefits both the plants and the soil. As a bonus, legumes have delicate flowers that add beauty and a pleasant aroma to your garden, and beans and peas can be eaten fresh, blanched and frozen for later consumption, and dried for use in soups and stews.

Peppers- Another favorite! Peppers are also members of the nightshade family, so you shouldn't plant them directly next to your tomatoes. The great thing about peppers is that they come in a style and flavor for every palate from the mild and sweet bell pepper, up to the hottest of chilies and reapers. The heat in a pepper is determined by its capsaicin content, which is found concentrated in the seeds, not in the flesh. A pepper's color is also not determined by the variety, but by how long it's left on the vine to ripen. You can pick them when they are green, but they will eventually turn to yellow, to orange, to red, if you let them.

Strawberries- These sweet perennial favorites are an edible member of the rose family, and they are a fantastic choice for urban gardening because of their versatility in growing conditions. You can put strawberry vines in pots, in hanging baskets, and in raised beds to act as a ground cover/living mulch for other plants. Even once they stop producing fruit for the season, the shiny foliage is interesting and attractive.

Herbs- Growing herbs in an urban garden is easy and fun! You can plant them nearly anywhere as standalone or companion plants, and they will thrive, although most herbs tend to be thirsty. The other great thing about herbs is that most are perennial, and if you grow them in small pots, you can bring them inside during the off-season and enjoy them year-round. Species like mints and basils also draw in beneficial insects and repel harmful ones, and sages and bergamots draw in pollinators, which are important for the health of your garden.

Begonias- With their shiny leaves and delicate, bright flowers, begonias are a terrific choice of annuals for your urban garden. These plants are hardy, fairly critter-resistant, and are always priced reasonably for any budget. They come in several colors, do not grow very tall, and work well in containers and raised beds for a pop of color and foliage texture.

Impatiens- These flowering annuals provide a lot of versatility in any garden. They are almost like goldfish- they will grow to the space you give them. Impatiens have unique red tints along their stems and will produce their signature four-petal flowers continuously in a wide variety of colors from mid- to late spring through early fall in a temperate climate. They can be planted in hanging baskets, as well, and they plant well in a mixture of other annuals.

Coleus- This foliage plant looks like something out of prehistory and comes in so many colors and patterns, it would be impossible to name them all. Coleus grows straight to a medium height, doesn't take up much horizontal space, is a fun accompaniment to flowering annuals, and will flower and go to seed late in the season, so if you don't want it self-seeding itself, you should remove it before it bolts.

Sweet potato vine- The flowering variety of sweet potato vine doesn't produce any food, but it is a lovely ornamental that can be used as ground cover, or in containers and hanging baskets. The dark, almost-black foliage and its lavender bell-shaped flowers are a nice contrast to break up the endless shades of green in any garden. They are hardy, drought-resistant, and tend to be left alone by most critters, save some deer.

Celosia- Celosia is a bright addition to an urban garden, and give containers and beds something with a fun texture to play off of. The rocket varieties of celosia (sometimes called cock's comb) are best suited for small spaces, and they grow in cone-shaped, feathery bursts of reds, oranges, and yellows. They are hardy and will bloom for the majority of a growing season, often lasting until after the first frost.

Snapdragons- Like rocket celosia, snapdragons add vertical texture and interest in container gardens. They come in a variety of bright and pastel colors for any taste, and for a little bit of an edge, leave them once the flowers have fallen- the foliage pattern left behind looks like little skulls. So funky!

Bulbs- It's entirely possible to add perennial bulbs to an urban garden, and they make a great choice along the outer edges of raised beds and to bring a pop of color to your containers in the early spring. You can choose bulbs like tulips, daffodils, and irises in raised beds, and smaller, more shallow-rooted bulbs like crocuses or grape hyacinth in containers.

Other annuals you might want to consider for your garden might be lobelia, marigolds, nasturtiums, petunias, pansies, and artemisia. These all can be planted in containers and do well in hot conditions. Once you've chosen all your varieties, you can actually get down to the business of gardening. Installing your seedlings is your next step, so let's go over some of the tools and techniques you'll need to get your garden from planned to planted!

Chapter 3: Planting and Maintenance Methods for Urban Settings

The nice thing about planting an urban garden is that you don't need too many bulky or long-handled tools. A good set of hand tools, like a trowel, hand rake, hand hoe or garden ax, bulb digger, and a weeding fork will set you up well for all your cultivation tasks. You'll also want a sturdy pair of gardening gloves, some utility scissors and twine, a bucket for weeding, and a basket of some sort for harvesting. You'll also need a hose or watering can, of course.

A good canvas bag should be all you need to tuck your tools away, and it's always recommended that you keep a garden journal. You can make notes about what's working and what isn't, which varieties you like or don't like, and jot down the dates of your planting, harvesting, and if you make any fertilizer or other applications to your soil. You should also have some stakes or cages on hand if you're growing any tomatoes or vining varieties of other species.

If you're planting in raised beds and haven't used enriched potting soil in your 50/50 mix, you'll want to do a little preparation before planting. You should get your hands on some straw or old newspaper (more likely in the city). Shred the newspaper and pile it into the beds, and then wet it down so it doesn't blow away. Do this every day for a few days until you can turn the decomposing newsprint into the soil. It will add much-needed organic material to your raised beds.

For planting exclusively in containers, you won't need to do any additional soil preparation since you've filled them with potting mix. When it's time to install your seedlings, you'll need your trowel and gloves. To make your life easier, you can lay out all your seedlings in their places before you start digging. When you remove seedlings from their pots or seedling cells, do so gently. Give the pot a squeeze to loosen the soil and then get a hold of the seedling at the base of the stem. A few good wiggles and you'll have it free. Holes should be dug a little wider and deeper than the pot the seedling was in.

Once your seedlings are free, give the roots a quick massage to break up any compaction. You don't need to remove all the original soil from the roots, as this is the soil they are used to, and it will ease their transition into your beds and pots. Place each seedling upright in its new home, and fill the hole around them, pressing lightly around the stem to make sure they stay standing straight. Once all your plants are where they need to be, water them generously and let them settle in.

"Water generously" is a phrase commonly associated with urban gardening. The nature of the urban heat island phenomenon, combined with the fact that containers and raised beds drain faster and retain less moisture than native soil means that you'll be doing a lot of watering. If you have a hose, that's great! You'll be done in no time. You can even consider putting drip irrigation or soaker hoses in a raised bed, to do your watering for you. These systems are fairly inexpensive and require running the tubing through the garden bed and setting your hose spigot on a timer. Sprinklers are not recommended for urban gardening, as they are not targeted enough and tend to wet the leaves, rather than the roots of the plants. This can lead to sunscald and pathogen issues. Best to use a hose.

For small balcony gardens, you can get by with a watering can, or you can put self-waterers in your containers. You can buy the glass bulbs, or you can make some from old beverage bottles; long-neck wine and spirit bottles work well and are durable, but plastic water and soda bottles can be used, too. The physics of this is simple- you fill the vessel and turn it upside-down into the soil. Water will only flow out of the bottle when the soil is dry enough for there to be pore space for the water. Once the soil is saturated, no more water can escape until the soil begins to dry out again. This technique can work in raised beds, too, if you are willing to use larger bottles and place them throughout the beds.

If you're not putting in a self-watering system of any kind, you should plan on watering every day, at least once a day. You should always water first thing in the morning, and if it's a particularly hot day, again in the evening once the sun has moved low in the sky. Urban gardens are thirsty gardens, and it's imperative that you keep the soil as evenly moist as you can by being a vigilant waterer. Of course, if you get a heavy rainstorm, you can skip that morning, but the point is more that staying proactive is better than having wilted plants that need to catch up. And again, water the roots, not the leaves to avoid moisture issues on your foliage.

Once you've established a good watering regimen, you're well on your way to garden success. The next things to worry about are the gardener's nemeses- weeds, pests, and pathogens. Heave a big sigh, it's okay. Let's talk about these problems in that order and get you set to tackle any issues that might head your way. It's important to know what to look for, how to handle concerns promptly, and how to avoid them in the future to be a better, more experienced gardener.

Weeds, thankfully, are not usually a terrible concern in a well-tended urban garden. Because you've imported your soil, you shouldn't have to worry about the weed seeds that lurk, dormant, in traditional native soil gardens. If you take care not to let weeds get ahead of you, manual weeding a couple of times each week should rid you of any pesky intruders. Another nice thing about weeds in containers and small raised beds is that they rarely have time to root very deeply and they are easily seen and plucked. You can also lay mulch in raised beds, if you're so inclined, by laying a barrier of plastic sheeting or old newspaper around the base of your plants.

That brings us to insect pests, and that can be an issue in urban gardening. This is because plants where they aren't expected, like the middle of a city, can draw in bugs that might normally not be there. Common garden pests include aphids and whiteflies, and these tiny invaders will eat almost anything green and growing. If you see them move in, especially on your vegetables, hose them off. A good blast of water is usually enough to shake them loose and send them to a watery grave. Alternatively, you can try a horticultural soap or oil.

What's Eating My Plant?
How to Recognize Common Pests by the Leaf Damage They Cause

Damage	Pest
Deformed leaves, sucking damage	Aphids
Discolored leaves, sucking damage	Thrips and mites
Chewed or skeletonized leaves	Beetles, caterpillars, and sawflies
Leaf galls (abnormal plant growths)	Cynipid wasps, certain aphids, psyllids, and mites
Leaf mines (white patterns on leaves)	Beetle, fly, or moth larvae
Folded leaves	Caterpillars, tree crickets, and spiders
Rolled leaves	Certain mites or some caterpillars
Chewed leaves, slime trails	Slugs and snails

- Knowing what's eating your pests can help you solve the problem quickly!
-

You can manually remove larger pests, like tomato hornworms and slugs (wear gloves!), or put out beer traps in the evenings. Other common pests to look for are vine borers and beetles. Sticky traps work well for these types of pests. Another thing to consider is hanging up a bird feeder or two. These will attract omnivorous birds who will help you out by eating the things that are eating your garden. You can also consider purchasing a clutch of ladybugs, who will help rid your plants of other, unwanted, insects.

Using biologic controls for insect pests is part of a horticultural practice known as IPM, or integrated pest management. It helps farmers and gardeners reduce the need to use harsh chemical insecticides and pesticides and maintain a healthier ecosystem. One last thing to consider is planting what's called a 'trap crop'. This is something that's particularly inviting to insect pests; for instance, flowering nettles are incredibly attractive to aphids. You could plant some in a pot off to the side and let the bugs feast on that, saving your other plants from harm. One of the best things you can do for your garden, though, is to be observant. If you take a close look at your plants every day, you are much more likely to see a problem at its very beginning stages and be able to nip it in the bud (pun intended!)

Pathogens are the last gardening concern we'll address in this segment, and because bacteria, viruses, and fungi are so widely varied, it would be difficult to talk about them all, so we'll go over some basics. One of the best ways to keep disease out of your garden is to keep being a proactive gardener. Plants have an immune system that is kept strong by being healthy, so when you follow best gardening practices, you are giving them the best chance to be disease-resistant. Keeping leaves dry, not over- or underwatering, and providing proper nutrition are great ways to help your garden avoid infection from pathogens.

Some common pathogens that can plague vegetables are early and late blight, blossom end rot, downy and powdery mildew, mosaic virus, and anthracnose. Some of these can also affect ornamentals, which can also be victims of leaf spots and vascular wilts. Again, best gardening practices should help you avoid any major issues, but some diseases have a way of sneaking in no matter how hard you try. If you see that your plants are in distress, first determine if they need water or a boost of fertilizer. Some heavy feeders will begin to droop mid-season, and a proper dose of a good organic fertilizer will help them perk back up. Be sure to follow dosing instructions to the letter.

While it's rarely seen in urban gardens, due to the soil used, nutrient toxicity can also present similarly to disease, with yellowed, curled leaves or 'rusty' spots. This likely isn't the case for you, but you can certainly take photos of your plant's unhappy spots and search online. No matter what, if you've got leaves and stems that are looking out of sorts, the best thing to do is to cut away all the diseased material and dispose of it in the trash, away from the garden. Clean your pruners or scissors with rubbing alcohol and hot, soapy water when you're done to avoid infecting another plant. If you have to, remove the entire affected plant. Keep a close eye on the plants around it, and if you must resort to using antibiotics or fungicides, be very mindful of applying them using proper doses and wearing gloves.

Take care not to splash any unaffected plants, you don't want to cause any collateral damage.

Now that you've got some solid basic knowledge of planting, watering, and maintaining your garden, let's talk about the future. In the next few segments, we'll cover how you can truly maximize your garden space and increase its productivity, how you can keep your garden and soil resting and happy in the off-season, and how to take your small concept from your patio to your community to bring the joy of fresh food and flowers to your neighborhood.

Chapter 4: Using Small Spaces to Your Advantage

Just because your gardening space is small, doesn't mean your gardening yield needs to be. We already talked about companion planting to maximize your horizontal space, so now let's go a little more in-depth about vertical gardening. We'll also take a look at succession planting, which can help you get more gardening out of less space by planting a second crop during a single growing season.

If you've incorporated hanging baskets into your gardening design, then you've already started vertical gardening. By utilizing another dimension of your gardening space, you can increase the yield of your garden. Trellises, stakes, and tomato cages are useful tools for training your plants to go up, not out, and they also keep delicate leaves from laying on damp soil, which encourages pathogens. Be creative about what you use for your vertical gardening. Anything can be a stake if you put your mind to it.

Picking the Right Method

Choose between these three different succession planting methods to help
your garden grow across the entire season:

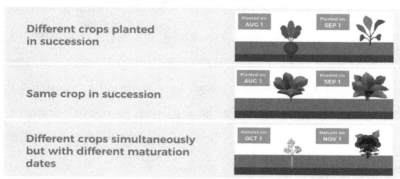

- Make the most of one season with succession planting -

Succession planting is another great way to make the most out of a small urban garden. If you live in a warm to temperate climate, you've got a growing season long enough to accommodate two fast-maturing crops. You can start with peas or beans in the early spring, and then put cucumber plants in the same space as the pea crop ends and the warmer part of summer begins. You can also plant the same crop in waves over the first month or so of the gardening season to have a continuous harvest all summer long.

Chapter 5: Planning for Continued Success

One of the things that's most important for the ongoing success of an urban garden is keeping the soil healthy. If you only have a few small pots, replacing the potting soil each year will not be a major expense. But if you've got raised beds or an entire patio's worth of containers, you want to be able to save that expense and re-use your soil. This means adding organic material and putting your garden to bed for the off-season.

Your easiest route to do this is to get some bagged compost and a big roll of burlap. If you have perennial herbs planted in your raised beds, cut them down to about two inches about the soil line, and bring the cuttings inside to dry and crumble for your spice cabinet. You should cut any other perennial flowers down to the soil level as well. Remove any other spent plant material from the bed, and spread a layer of compost over the whole bed. Then roll out some burlap and stake it down, and you've tucked your bed in for the winter! When spring comes, turn the soil over to start the preparation process all over again. Remember, you can never have too much organic matter in your garden.

For your containers, you can do one of a couple of things. You can mix some compost into all of your pots and give them a little burlap lid for the winter- just cut a square, lay it over the pot, and tie a bit of twine around the outside to secure it-, or you can bag your soil in big contractor bags, layering in compost as you go. Then tie the bags up with as little air in them as possible, and set them someplace safe for the winter. Just pop the soil back in your pots and get back to business in the spring.

You can spend the off-season going through your journal notes and making plans for the following year. Check out seed and plant catalogs and decide if you want to try any different varieties or methods, and take a gander at gadgets made for small-scale gardening. You can jot down anything that piques your interest and snag deals on off-season sales and pre-sales. The research and the new toys are both parts of the fun of gardening, so enjoy!

Chapter 6: Community Gardening Considerations

One last note about urban gardening pertains to having a community garden. If you are interested in having a larger garden with your neighbors or building mates, you should check with the proper authorities to make sure you've got permission to use a shared space or community property. Community gardens are a great way to make sure that everyone has fresh food and beautiful flowers to brighten their lives all growing season.

Once you've made sure that it's okay to have a community garden, you can set some protocols in place to ensure that everyone knows the rules. Have a list of 'members' and divvy up time slots to make sure the work gets done. You can divide tasks up by days or weeks, and put a system in place so people get their fair share of the harvest. Have fun making friends and building a sense of community spirit! If you've got an overabundance, don't forget to share with a local food pantry or soup kitchen, to spread the love a little farther.

PART III

Raised Bed Gardening

Are you thinking about building a garden, but you don't have the time, space, or inclination to till up a patch of open ground? Maybe you've always wanted to grow fresh, healthy food or beautiful flowers at home, but you've got mobility concerns or physical limitations that won't allow you to bend and twist in a traditional garden. Or maybe you live on a rental property where you want a garden, but it can't be a permanent installation. No worries! You can be a gardener, and you can do it with raised beds!

Raised bed gardens are a great way to address any of these restrictions, and with the development of compact varieties of many common garden plants, you can grow almost anything you'd normally see in a traditional native soil garden. By definition, a raised bed garden is any garden that utilizes materials to create a planting space that sits above the elevation of the ground, and the only limit on what you can build is your imagination. Raised bed gardens can be built from a variety of materials, eliminate much of the guesswork of soil quality, and will provide a rewarding hobby you'll enjoy for years to come.

Chapter 1: Designing and Building a Raised Bed Garden

Before you can plant a raised bed garden, you've got to build a raised bed garden, and that means finding a great spot and selecting a design. Since most flowers and herbs require about six hours of sun a day, and six hours is the absolute minimum of sunlight for vegetables, the first thing you need to consider is finding a well-lit spot for your garden beds.

The next thing that comes into play when choosing a site for a raised bed garden is the slope. You want to choose a site that is level, can be leveled, or can be terraced. While a gentle slope is good for drainage, a more dramatic slope can be an invitation for erosion and runoff, even in a contained bed. You should also take into consideration any trees that are nearby. While they might not cast shade now, is there a possibility that they may grow and block the sun from your garden in the future?

A third consideration for raised bed gardens is their proximity to a water source. Because raised beds tend to be warmer and have more drainage than a traditional in-ground garden, they can be thirsty. You want to make sure you've got convenient access to water so you don't have to travel far to fulfill your garden's watering needs. It's easy to water when the hose is right there, and it's easier to put off when you don't feel like dragging that hose all over every day.

Once you've chosen a site that best fits your criteria, it's time to think about your design. Creating a raised bed garden is fun because the possibilities are endless. Some things to think about when you're designing your garden are bed dimensions, bed height, bed arrangement, and what materials you'd like to use. Keep in mind that you can build raised beds from hardwood, masonry block, PVC vinyl, or composite materials. You can also take advantage of the many commercially available pre-fabricated kits to create your garden design.

When considering dimensions, keep in mind that if you are gardening for food, you need about 200 sq. feet per person in the household throughout a growing season. If you're going to garden for flowers or a mix of food and flowers, you can go crazy with whatever dimensions you'd like. The key is to make sure that your beds are deep enough to support the roots of your growing plants, with 12 inches being a standard minimum. Using good old-fashioned pencil and paper, sketch a few ideas. You can go with a set of squares arranged in a quadrant, or some rectangles set in rows like a traditional garden. Think about using shapes like triangles to fill in corner spaces, or building adjacent boxes in increasing heights like steps to create a more interesting space and accommodate plants of different heights.

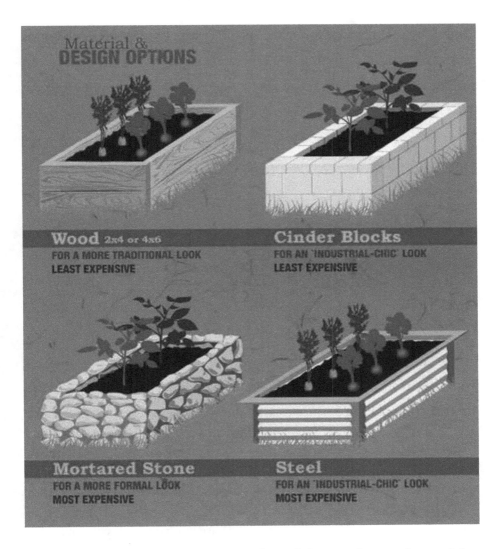

Material & DESIGN OPTIONS

Wood 2x4 or 4x6
FOR A MORE TRADITIONAL LOOK
LEAST EXPENSIVE

Cinder Blocks
FOR AN 'INDUSTRIAL-CHIC' LOOK
LEAST EXPENSIVE

Mortared Stone
FOR A MORE FORMAL LOOK
MOST EXPENSIVE

Steel
FOR AN 'INDUSTRIAL-CHIC' LOOK
MOST EXPENSIVE

- Raised beds can be designed in a variety of shapes, sizes, and materials -

If you've got mobility issues, you might want to think about raised growing tables rather than beds. These can be constructed from wood, or you can purchase them in composite vinyl. These are large troughs on legs or stilts, often with locking casters to roll them into different positions. The troughs have drainage built into the underside, and are generally deep enough for many common garden plants, although you might be hard-pressed to grow root vegetables in them. Raised tables are a great way to make gardening adaptive to people of any physical capability. You should also think about what else you'd like to have in your garden to make it an inviting space. You can hang bird feeders, a table and chairs, or some whimsical gnomes. You want to brainstorm how to make your garden a place you'll enjoy working and relaxing in.

If you are going to be building your own beds, then you should look into repurposed materials. Contact any friends in the construction trades, and see if they have any leftovers you can have for cheap or the price of hauling. You can also look at your local online buy/sell/trade groups and see if anyone is selling or giving away construction materials. Sometimes, you can get discount 'cut ends' from the sawmill or lumberyard- these are pieces cut from larger planks that the contractor didn't need. The only material to avoid is pressure-treated lumber, it can leach the treatment chemicals into your garden soil, which can affect the nutrient balance and damage plant roots. Be resourceful and you'll be able to find a plethora of materials for the taking without spending a ton of money.

When it's time to build, you should make sure you've got all your materials and tools in place. Consider everything you need to measure, cut, and assemble your beds, including hardware for wooden, vinyl, and composite beds, and mortar for masonry block beds. Keep in mind the old adage to measure twice and cut once to avoid waste. If you've got a square and a level on hand, they can be invaluable tools for making sure you're on the right track for having nice, even beds. Of course, if you're handy enough to be building your own raised beds, you already know all these things!

If you've purchased pre-fabricated garden kits, make sure you open the packages, look at the directions and material lists, and ensured that all the parts and hardware are there BEFORE you start putting anything together. These kits don't generally require too many tools for assembly, but you'll probably need a screwdriver or power drill with screwdriver bits, or a wrench or rachet if it assembles with nuts and bolts. If anything is missing, contact the manufacturer to let them know. You will also want to have a level on hand for when you set your new bed into place. You should stow any paperwork, including assembly instructions, in a file for safekeeping. You may need to replace worn-out hardware in the future, and having the original paperwork will save you time and potentially money when purchasing new fasteners.

Once your beds are built, the next thing you are going to need is soil. In a traditional garden, you have to work with what you've got, amending as you go to reach optimal conditions. In a raised bed garden, you get to choose the soil and avoid some of that preparation. If you can, you should have your soil delivered in bulk from a reputable supplier. When you order, you should specify that you are going to be using the soil for gardening and that you want screened topsoil, preferably pH tested and irradiated for weeds. You want to make sure you are getting quality for your money. The supplier can help you calculate how much soil you need based on the dimensions of your beds.

When your soil is delivered, try to have it dumped as close to your beds as possible, without ruining your lawn, of course. If you can't install all your soil in one day, make sure to cover the pile with a tarp or sheet of plastic. You don't want a sudden overnight rain shower to wash all your soil away!

If you cannot get soil delivered in bulk, you can purchase bagged topsoil, but be careful about the quality. Bagged topsoil can be heavy, wet, and prone to mold. If you do go with a bagged option, make sure you fill your beds slowly, giving time between layers for the previous layer to dry out a bit before you continue.

With your beds full of soil, it's time to make them fertile! Before you plant anything, you need to add some organic matter to perk up the soil organisms that just found themselves unceremoniously dumped in a new home. You can spread a layer of compost on your beds, and turn it into the soil, or you can lay some straw (not hay!) on top of the soil and give it a good wet-down. Water the straw layer every day for a few days to encourage decomposition, and then turn it into the soil to continue to break down. You can never, repeat, never, have enough organic matter in your garden soil. Finish your soil preparation by applying some granulated or liquid all-purpose fertilizer, being sure to closely follow the packaging instructions. If you've got any questions about this, contact your local Farm Bureau or Cooperative Extension for guidance before you apply anything.

Chapter 2: Choosing Plant Varieties That Thrive in Raised Beds

When you are selecting plants for raised beds, you want to make sure that you choose varieties that are compatible with growing both outside of native soil and in a compact area. Whether you are planting vegetables, flowers, herbs, or a combination of the three, you want to look for plants that are labeled as compact, dwarf, or 'good for containers', before you read anything else on the plant tag. Yes, the plant tag. When growing in raised beds, at least for the first year until you build up your soil, it's best to start with seedlings and plant starts rather than from seed. It will make your transition from having no garden to having a freshly-built raised bed garden easier. Skipping the home-sowing step will let you go from zero to planting in no time, and with the limited space available in a raised bed garden, transplanting nursery stock or seedlings takes the guesswork out of planting.

Let's takes a look at the information you will find on a plant tag, so you know what to look for to choose what's right for your garden:

- Hardiness zone

- The hardiness zone, or growing zone, is the region or subregion that is optimal for each type of plant. You can find your hardiness zone in the United States on the USDA website. Most summer gardening plants are rated for the majority of temperate climates, but it's always nice to be sure before you plant something.

- Plant name- common and botanical

- A plant tag will include the common and the botanical (scientific) name of the species and variety. Sometimes you might see a third component to the name, that is most likely a cultivar. Cultivars are just a further sub-variety of a specific species and may indicate a different color or size from its parent species.

- Picture and description of the mature plant

- This is self-explanatory. It's just nice to see what your end result should look like, or what size the flowers, fruit, or vegetables are going to be.

- Planting and spacing instructions

- Knowing how to plant your seedlings and how you should space them is crucial information. You know best the dimensions of your garden, and when you're choosing seedling and starts, don't buy too many! Remember that these tiny shoots will become full-size plants over the coming months, and they will need room to grow, expand, and breathe. This is why compact varieties are best for raised beds, especially for growing vegetables. You can also grow up rather than out, and we'll go over vertical gardening before this chapter is over.

- Raised bed gardening is a great way to intermingle flowers, herbs, and vegetables in a limited space, so be sure to choose a range of different plants. We'll talk about companion planting in the next section so you can arrange all your varieties to maximize pollination, keep your soil healthy, and avoid pest infestations.

- Days to bloom/days to harvest

- Another piece of useful information you'll find on a seedling tag is how long it will take you to see your first flowers or food. This can help you make decisions about which varieties you want to plant and give you a guideline to help determine if your plants are maturing on schedule. If they're not, it's an indication that you need to do some troubleshooting. This bit of information should also include if your plants are short-blooming, long-blooming, single-harvest, or continuous harvest. This is something else to take into consideration when you choose your varieties.

- Sun requirements

- Part of being a successful gardener is giving your plants the best environment to encourage proper growth. A big part of this is making sure they're getting the recommended amount of light. Most veggies and herbs require a minimum of 6 hours of sun each day, while some ornamental species do better in partial and full shade. Knowing these requirements will help you choose varieties and put the right plant in the right place.

- Water requirements

- Most plant tags will also tell you how thirsty a plant is, which can help you decide which plants to install. Keep in mind that most gardens require approximately four inches of water each week, and that total should be slightly higher for raised beds because they usually drain faster than a native soil garden. If you've got problem areas where water pools or you're on a slight slope, you can get thirstier plants or plants that tolerate wet conditions to put in those spots. In that way, you can make the most of every inch of your limiter raised bed space.

- Indication of heirloom/ hybrid/ GMO or non-GMO

- On your seedling tags, you will find it noted whether a plant variety is an heirloom, a hybrid, or GMO/non-GMO. To choose between these options, let's take a quick look at what these terms mean. Heirloom varieties are true to species. New plants are grown from seed that is the exact genetic material as the generations of plants that came before it. Hybrid varieties are those that have been carefully crossbred by botanists to exhibit the desirable traits of two or more heirloom varieties. The characteristics of these plants can fluctuate from generation to generation because they can exhibit recessive genes.

- GMO stands for 'genetically modified organism'. These varieties haven't been bred to exhibit characteristics, they have been changed on a genetic level to eliminate bad traits and emphasize good ones. GMOs were developed for several reasons, not the least of which was to modify corn to be easier to grow in arid climates, and the popular Flavr Savr tomato, which had its ripening compounds inhibited to have a longer shelf life. GMO/non-GMO has become an ongoing argument in the past two decades, and there are proponents for both sides. You can decide on your own if you want to grow GMO varieties, but I encourage you to do some research before you purchase plants.

Once you have a basic understanding of how to read plant tags, you can begin to choose the varieties you want to grow. If you are focusing on gardening for food, you should choose compact versions of some easy-to-grow favorites to get you started.

Beans/peas- Beans and peas are legumes, which are enormously beneficial to the health of your soil. These plants return much-needed nitrogen to the soil as they grow, and they can be planted next to your heavy-feeding vegetables to prevent the stripping of nutrients. There are some fantastic bush varieties of all your favorite beans and peas available, but if you must have the climbing varieties, check out the section on vertical gardening later in this chapter.

Cucumbers/Melons- Cucumbers are a versatile plant to have in your raised bed garden because they are medium feeders, grow quickly, and the fruit can be used fresh or pickled for use later. They are a member of the cucurbit family, as are melons. You can find compact or bush varieties of cucumbers and melons, eliminating a tangle of vines and providing you with cool, refreshing produce from mid-summer through fall. One note, cucurbits require a lot of water to promote proper growth, as the ripe fruit has very high water content.

Peppers, Tomatoes, and Eggplants- You might not be aware that these three species are in the same plant family, as are the humble potato. This is the nightshade family, and they are garden staples worldwide. These plants are easy to grow and maintain, but they are heavy feeders and will strip your soil if you aren't careful. You can fertilize mid-season (more on fertilizer in a bit) and make sure they've got lots of organic material to supplement their feed. These plants should also not be planted next to each other in the garden, to alleviate an attack from nightshade-loving pests and to keep your soil healthier.

Asparagus- Adding asparagus to a raised bed garden is a choice that will teach you patience and self-control. Asparagus is loosely related to the lily family, and it is a perennial. This means that once you plant it, it will take a couple of years to establish itself, but cared for properly, it will continue to work in your garden for up to thirty years! The patience and self-control come from being able to resist eating those tender green shoots until you reach year three. Good luck!

Strawberries- A perennial fruit, strawberries are also a perennial favorite. Strawberries are actually part of the rose family, and you can find terrific compact varieties to put in your raised bed garden. You can also consider standard varieties to wind through the beds as living ground cover. Once you plant some strawberries, you can enjoy their fragrant flowers and their tasty fruit for up to ten years before they need to be replaced.

Blueberries- Compact blueberry bushes have become popular in recent years and for good reason. These plump berries are rich in nutrients and antioxidants, making them a breakfast and snacking favorite. The one catch with planting blueberries is this- they do prefer a more acidic soil than most fruits and vegetables. However, if you've got one problem corner of your garden, where you know the drainage isn't quite right, it gets a little shade, or any other tiny glitch, you can isolate a berry bush or two in that spot and give it some acid plant food to help it thrive without acidifying the rest of your soil.

Herbs- Herbs are the epitome of edible gardening, aren't they? You can plant herbs among your fruits and veggies and watch them grow and flower, repel insects, and the best part, make tasty accompaniments to all your favorite foods. It's great to be able to walk outside and snip off some fresh basil or oregano to toss into your dinner recipe. (Note: the difference between herbs and spices is that 'herbs' refer to seasonings made from the foliage of the plant, and 'spices' refer to seasoning made from any other part, such as the seeds, stems, bark, roots, etc.)

You can easily add ornamental plants to a raised bed garden to add interest, draw pollinating insects, and repel pests. There is a vast array of ornamental plants and your personal aesthetic sense may dictate what you plant, here is a list of good starter ornamentals that do well in a raised bed, and how you can interplant them as companions to your food plants.

French marigolds- Marigolds are an easy-to-maintain annual that come in a variety of colors and sizes. French marigolds are among the hardiest and there are several cultivars that do well in raised beds, such as Queen Sophia and Honeycomb. French marigolds (which actually originated in Central America) are drought-resistant, repel deer, and don't have much odor, although their color draws in bees and other pollinators.

Rudbeckia and echinacea- You may know these perennial wildflowers more commonly as black-eyed Susans and coneflowers. These are terrific pollinator plants and help prevent soil erosion with their strong roots. You can interplant them with your vegetables and herbs to create a strong ecosystem. There are many compact varieties available that will work well in raised beds.

Daffodils- Another perennial, this time a bulb. Daffodils are easy to grow, pleasant to look at, and best of all, deer-resistant. A perimeter of daffodils will bloom in the mid-to-late spring and protect your tender young seedlings from being nibbled by four-legged pests. One note about daffodils- once they are established, they will begin to spread. You can divide the bulbs every few years and transplant them elsewhere or give them away.

Calendula- This annual is technically an herb, but the flowers are beautiful and beneficial. They attract both pollinating and predatory insects, and their sticky sap traps unwanted pests like aphids and whiteflies. In warmer hardiness zones, calendula can be left in the garden over the winter as a cover crop.

Nasturtium- Also an annual herb, nasturtium has several beneficial properties. It grows low to the ground and acts as a natural mulch, its foliage is unique and provides an interesting texture, and it has a strong (not unpleasant) odor that repels pests. In addition, both the flowers and the foliage are edible.

German chamomile- If you like a delicate aesthetic, you'll love German chamomile in your garden. This self-sowing annual has tiny, sweetly-scented flowers that bring in pollinators and beneficial insects. You can leave the plants in the garden over the winter to prevent erosion and add organic material to the soil.

Most, if not all of the above fruits, vegetables, herbs, and ornamental plants will grow in warm to temperate hardiness zones. If you are in a tropical or cold zone where the growing season is much longer or shorter, you should investigate varieties of these plants that thrive in your particular zone.

Chapter 3: Easy Planting and Maintenance Techniques

Once you've chosen your plants, you'll need to get them installed into your raised beds. For planting and everyday maintenance techniques, there are some basic tools you'll need and want to have on hand. These include:

- trowel, hand rake, and weeding fork

- bulb digger

- short-handled pitchfork

- garden hoe or garden ax

- sturdy gloves

- weeding bucket

- harvest basket

- utility scissor/knife and twine

- hand pruners

- watering can or hose

- stakes or trellises for unruly plants

- tool storage shed or trunk

- a garden journal or journaling software application

Having the proper tools on hand will make any gardening task easier. If you're on a budget, check around at rummage sales and online in your local buy/sell/trade groups for bargains on second-hand tools. You can also take advantage of end-of-season clearance sales at garden centers and home improvement stores. You should use your journal from beginning to end of the season to mark down what you're planting, what products you've applied (fertilizer, compost, pesticides, etc.), how much you harvest, and other notes that will help you with dissecting and assessing the season and planning for next year.

Planting Your Seedlings

When it's time to get your plants installed in your raised beds, you want to make sure you arrange them in a way that will be the most beneficial. If you are installing any perennials, you should choose their location first, and build around them. You want to make sure you aren't placing your heavy feeders, like the nightshades, next to each other. Split them up with herbs, legumes, and your flowers, and cucurbits. This will help naturally with pest control and will discourage your soil from becoming stripped of its nutrient load.

To physically plant your seedlings, you'll want to make a hole that is deeper and wider than the pot or seedling cell that they are currently in. For small plants, you can use a bulb digger to make even holes. Be sure to use the spacing instructions on the plant tag so your seedlings have room to spread, grow, and have adequate airflow. You should give the pots or cells a squeeze to loosen up the soil and then grasp the seedling at the base of the stem and give it a good wiggle to release it from the pot.

Once the plants are free, gently massage the soil and roots to loosen them up and place them in your holes. Fill in the holes and lightly tamp down the soil around the base of the plant. When all your plants are installed, give the bed a good watering and leave the plants to settle into their new homes. Don't fiddle with them unless they look seriously askew, they will need a few days for their roots to reach out and establish themselves in their new soil. Place the plant tags in the garden to remind you which plants are which, or use a permanent marker and plastic spoons or knives to make your own plant markers.

Watering for Maximum Plant Health

One of the most important functions of a gardener is to provide water for their plants. You have taken responsibility for growing plants where none were growing before, and you must give them the necessities to thrive. I might go so far as to say that watering properly can be the make-or-break key to any garden. Cultivated plants require approximately four inches of water a week to maintain health and promote growth. You need to be able to meet those needs to be successful.

You should plan on watering your garden every day, except if you have had or anticipate heavy rain. Many people choose to water by hand with a hose or watering can, but raised bed gardens are the perfect set-up for adding drip irrigation or soaker hose system. If your hose spigot is close to your garden, these can be a relatively inexpensive way to make sure you are watering enough, and they are simple to set up.

Soaker hoses and drip irrigation work by delivering water directly to your soil and the roots of your plants. Soaker hoses are the more 'primitive' of the technology. These are hoses, capped on the far end, made of permeable material that you split and run from your spigot, through your beds, and cover with a light coating of soil. When the faucet is opening, water flows through the hose's permeable sides and into your garden. A simple timer added to your spigot can make a world of difference in having well-watered, happy plants. A drip irrigation system is similar but more targeted. Instead of being a permeable hose, there are tubes or hoses with holes that can be placed directly near the base of your plants. Both systems are available in DIY kits.

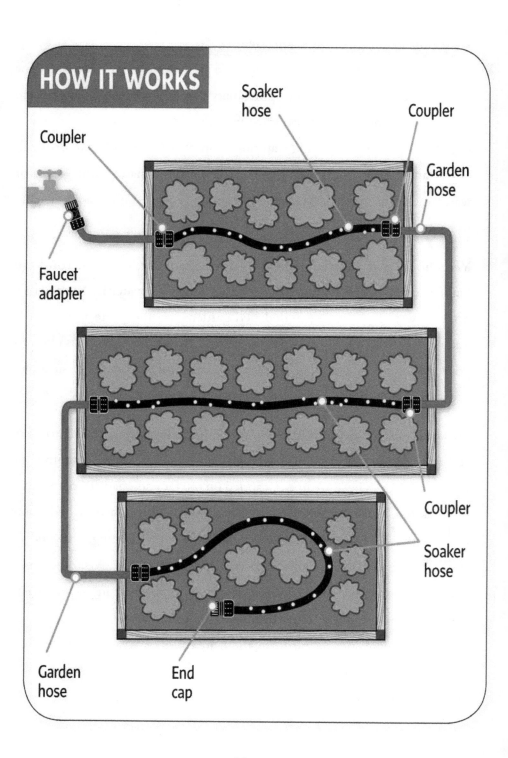

HOW IT WORKS

Coupler

Soaker hose

Coupler

Garden hose

Faucet adapter

Coupler

Soaker hose

Garden hose

End cap

96

- A simple DIY soaker hose system can ensure your garden is adequately watered -

If you are watering with a hose or can, be sure to always water the roots, not the leaves. You don't want your plants to get sunscald or invite pathogens to move in on wet foliage. No matter how you choose to water, a rain gauge is a good addition to any garden. They come in a ton of designs from industrial to whimsical, and they are helpful in showing gardeners of all abilities how much natural moisture your garden is receiving. You'll be surprised. Sometimes the hardest downpours don't shed as much volume as a light rain that lasts hours.

Fertilizer and Compost for Optimum Growth

Gardening in raised beds poses a unique challenge in soil health. While you may not have needed to do an initial soil test based on your supplier, you will need to do a little work to keep that soil healthy throughout your first year and beyond, because you don't want to have the expense of replacing the soil frequently. You can accomplish healthy soil year after year by liberal use of compost and discerning use of fertilizers.

You cannot ever add too much organic material to your soil, and compost is a fantastic way to achieve this. Whether you make your own or purchase bagged or bulk compost, you can add a layer to your beds at any time and it will never be too much. Compost is made up of decomposed plant matter and food scraps which is chock full of beneficial microorganisms. It helps create a thriving soil ecosystem in your garden. When you have more healthy organisms in your soil, your garden will retain more moisture, and have better soil pore space which allows for the movement of air and water to the roots and lets the roots spread for sturdier plants.

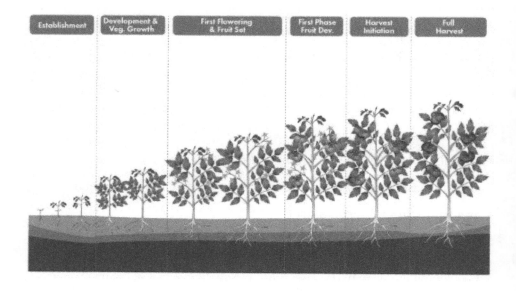

- Understanding the life cycle of your vegetables will help you know if you need fertilizer -

Fertilizer is a great tool for encouraging continued growth in heavy feeders and alleviating the drain of nutrients for your soil. However, fertilizer isn't a panacea and should be used sparingly and correctly. Too much of it will cause toxicity of nitrogen, phosphorus, and potassium (the big three nutrients), and too much phosphorus running off from your garden into the water table can contribute to larger environmental concerns.

When you use fertilizer partly through the growing system to supplement the nutrition in your garden, it is called 'side-dressing'. Be sure to follow all directions on your fertilizer package closely. If your product needs to be diluted, be sure to do so in the proper amount of water. Spray (or sprinkle) only near the roots of the plants you want to fertilize, because you don't want to encourage weed growth, either. If you have any questions about fertilizer application, you should call or email your local Cooperative Extension office or Farm Bureau. You will find someone there who can help you decipher your needs.

Dealing with Weeds, Pests, and Pathogens

One thing all gardeners have to deal with are unwanted visitors in our garden spaces. Weed, insect pests, furry critters, and pathogens are always lurking, looking for vulnerabilities to exploit. So how can you protect your plants from these invaders? Let's take a look at weeds first.

Weeds are plant matter that pops up in your garden, unplanted and uninvited. Of course, it's been said that to identify a weed, you must first know the heart of the gardener and the intent of the garden. That being said, I don't know too many people who cultivate crabgrass. Manual weeding is always an option, and some people love weeding, saying it's a great task for exercise and mental catharsis. I'm not one of those people, so here are some tips on avoiding and alleviating weeds in your raised beds:

1- Fill the space with plants you want. Don't give weeds any room to move in. Happy, healthy plants won't let too many weeds move into their territory. Use companion plants that will act as ground covers and choke out weeds before they can grow too large.

2- Mulch! If you can't cover the soil with plants, cover it with mulch. This could be grass clippings, straw, leaves, plastic or cloth weed-blocker, or traditional wood chips, although I would caution that chips should be your last choice in a raised bed garden. They don't break down quickly into the soil which could cause you issues in later seasons.

3- Reduce tilling. Weed seed likes to hide dormant in the soil and weeds begin to show up when the soil is turned, exposing them. While it is a good idea to aerate your soil with regular cultivation, it's not recommended to continuously turn over your soil exposing those weed seeds. Try to reduce your tilling to preparatory work at the beginning of the season and maybe perform a second tillage in the fall, to turn in the last shreds of spent plant material.

4- Herbicides. This should be your last resort, for a couple of reasons. First, if you are growing food, you want to be careful about spraying these chemicals on plants you intend to consume. Second, most commercially-available herbicides are not discriminatory, meaning they will kill all plant life they come in contact with, not just your weeds.

While weeds are a major concern for most gardeners, another thing to keep an eye out for is insects. Not all insects are harmful, so how can you know the difference? Well, if it's eating your plant, it's harmful, and if it's eating the insect eating the plant, it's beneficial. You want to be able to draw beneficial insects to your garden for this purpose and for pollination, and also be able to identify any harmful insects so you can take action before they can cause too much damage.

Like herbicides, heavy pesticide usage is not recommended for food gardens. There are several alternatives to using chemical pesticides in the garden, including horticultural soaps and oils, attracting beneficial insects and birds to eat the harmful pests, and in some cases, washing away the pests with a strong jet from your hose; this is a useful approach to ridding yourself of aphids and whiteflies. Try hanging a bird feeder to bring in omnivorous birds to chow down on your insect pests. You can also purchase large clutches of ladybugs to release in your garden to help with harmful insect control.

In the case of large bugs like tomato hornworms or vine-boring beetles, you can remove the pests manually and dispatch them as you see fit. You can also try sticky traps for whiteflies and larger beetle species, like Japanese beetles. For slugs and snails, use up the old beer in your refrigerator by placing the brew in shallow dishes in the garden overnight. They will help themselves to a drink, and there will be no survivors. If you're having a hard time identifying a bug, take a photo and search online. If that doesn't wield any definitive answers, email the photo to your local Cooperative Extension or Farm Bureau- they have staff and volunteers who are trained to assist with these types of questions.

The best way to stop insect issues is to be observant. Take care to look at your garden every day and note any changes like foliage and vines being eaten. Look for slug trails and insect frass (poop) on or under the leaves. Being vigilant is your best defense against pest issues. If you have tried everything and you're in need of using a pesticide, try to use organic products, especially on food plants. When all else fails and you find you have to use any pesticides, make sure you follow all label directions to the letter. You don't want to contaminate your food or the environment, and you definitely don't want to cause yourself any physical injury.

If your pest problem isn't bugs, but woodland creatures, there are a few approaches you can take to humanely deal with the problem. If small burrowers like chipmunks, rabbits, and voles are your culprits, try sonic stakes in the ground around your raised beds. These are usually solar-powered and are available at many garden centers or online. The stakes emit a high-frequency tone that isn't able to be heard by the human ear, but drives underground rodents nuts. For larger munchers, like deer, groundhogs, skunks, and raccoons, consider putting netting or fencing around your beds, and spray a pheromone-based repellant around the perimeter of your garden area.

That leads us to the third bane of the gardener's existence, and that is plant pathogens. While gardeners want to encourage all the helpful bacteria that live in the soil, they also need to avoid the harmful microorganisms that live on plants. These can be fungi, bacteria, or viruses, and the number one thing you can do to avoid infestation is to have proper airflow in your garden. Dry leaves are happy leaves. Microorganisms love to find wet, dark places to thrive. Keep your garden airy and your foliage dry to discourage colonies from forming.

Just like people, plants have an immune system that protects them from disease. If the plants are healthy and happy, they will be less prone to infection, so just by following best practices, you can help your plants stay free of disease. You should also be mindful of any 'wounds' on your plant-these can become infected just like a cut on human skin. Take care when pruning or harvesting to only remove plant material at the natural joints to avoid any opening that could invite infection.

If you find that an infection has moved in on your plants, the first thing you should do is remove the affected part of the plant or the entire plant, if necessary. Don't compost diseased plant material, dispose of it in the trash. You don't want to encourage the harmful organisms to breed in your compost pile and end up back in your soil later. The most common plant pathogens that you will see in a home garden are powdery and downy mildew, anthracnose, early and late blight, blossom end rot, and mosaic virus. Like with insect pests, you're going to want to be observant. Many times, you can save a plant or plant population by catching the disease and removing the diseased portion without losing the whole plant. This is another reason it's so important to keep plants of the same family separate in the garden. You don't want powdery mildew to affect all your cucurbits or blight hitting all your nightshades.

If you find that you must use more aggressive methods to get rid of pathogens, be smart about your approach. You can get a wide variety of organic fungicides, antivirals, and antibiotics to treat your plants, but always be sure to follow all instructions to the letter and use personal protective equipment if it's indicated. One note about using these products in a home garden: most vegetable plants are annuals and only have one life cycle. If a plant is so diseased that you think commercial remedies are necessary, it's probably just easier to throw away the plant and try again next year. It's better to expend your time and money saving valuable perennials if you must use disease-killing products.

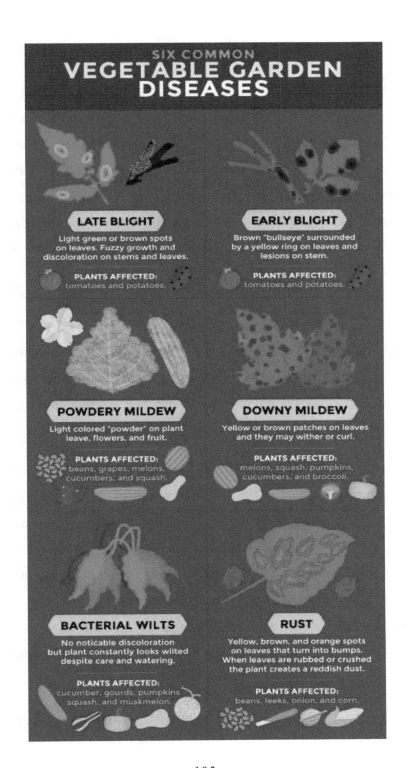

SIX COMMON
VEGETABLE GARDEN DISEASES

LATE BLIGHT

Light green or brown spots on leaves. Fuzzy growth and discoloration on stems and leaves.

PLANTS AFFECTED:
tomatoes and potatoes.

EARLY BLIGHT

Brown "bullseye" surrounded by a yellow ring on leaves and lesions on stem.

PLANTS AFFECTED:
tomatoes and potatoes.

POWDERY MILDEW

Light colored "powder" on plant leave, flowers, and fruit.

PLANTS AFFECTED:
beans, grapes, melons, cucumbers, and squash.

DOWNY MILDEW

Yellow or brown patches on leaves and they may wither or curl.

PLANTS AFFECTED:
melons, squash, pumpkins, cucumbers, and broccoli.

BACTERIAL WILTS

No noticable discoloration but plant constantly looks wilted despite care and watering.

PLANTS AFFECTED:
cucumber, gourds, pumpkins squash, and muskmelon.

RUST

Yellow, brown, and orange spots on leaves that turn into bumps. When leaves are rubbed or crushed the plant creates a reddish dust.

PLANTS AFFECTED:
beans, leeks, onion, and corn.

- Being vigilant will help you identify issues and handle them before they explode -

I can't impress upon you enough how much vigilance and observation are key to identifying and eliminating pests and pathogens in your raised beds. It's also important to follow best gardening practices and do things that will invite helpful organisms, like good bacteria in the soil and beneficial pollinators and predator insects to control the pest population. This practice is known as IPM, or integrated pest management, and it helps you build not just a thriving garden, but a thriving ecosystem.

Chapter 4: Maximize Space with Vertical Growing

If you have your heart set on growing things that don't come in favorable compact varieties, or if you just want to maximize the space in your raised beds, you can utilize vertical growing to suit your needs. Vertical growing is precisely what it sounds like, and it can be easy and fun!

You can use almost anything your heart desires as a trellis or support, and it's entirely up to budget and taste. One great idea I've seen over the years is using a repurposed children's soccer practice net- you know, those square string grids on a metal frame. It was set in the center of a raised bed with peas and beans climbing it. You can make something similar with just a few lengths of lumber and some sturdy twine. You can also use the handles from old tools (broken rakes, anyone?), tomato cages used both narrow and wide side down, and bits of lumber like one-inch furring strips. Be creative!

Another vertical idea is to place tall shepherd's hooks in the corner of your garden to hang pots on to drape the plants downward, or to build a four-corner frame, like a four-poster canopy bed to fit the dimensions of your bed. You can grow things up all the legs and along the beams to get a ton of growing space that you didn't have before. So, what can you grow vertically? Anything vining variety! This means you could free up valuable horizontal space by growing your cucumbers, melons, strawberries, peas, and beans, as well as vining ornamentals, on trellises and supports. The only requirement is using materials sturdy enough to hold those plants once they begin to get heavy with fruit and flowers. And of course, a step stool, if you need one. I once had to harvest cucumbers out of my dogwood after a particularly ambitious vine surpassed its trellis, the stockade fence beyond it, and began to climb the tree!

Chapter 5: Harvesting and Overwintering

Growing and maintaining a garden is great, but getting to harvest and enjoy the things you've grown is even better. When you grow your own food and flowers, you can always have a home full of fresh beautiful things. Because how you harvest is important as when you harvest, let's go over some basics for both food plants and ornamentals so you make the most out of your garden while it's at its peak.

When you cut flowers for bouquets or arrangements, it is always best to cut the stem at a length longer than you need- you can always trim the excess later. Try to cut at a joint or at the base of the stem, and always use a pair of sharp hand pruners or utility scissors to make a clean cut. You should also make sure your cuts are on the diagonal. This lets the plant heal faster and gives the cut end a larger surface to take up water from your vase or floral foam. Have fun arranging your cut flowers! It's such an easy way to brighten a room or brighten someone else's day! A birthday bouquet is that much more special when the flowers are homegrown.

For harvesting your food crops, you should refer back to the information on your plant tags, which will let you know approximately when you should expect to have your first pickable crops. Some varieties will continue to fruit for the entire rest of the season, as long as you harvest, they will keep producing. Some are more of a one-and-done crop and will give you their harvest and then begin to fade. Once your garden begins to get close to the mark for beginning to harvest, then you should keep an eye out every day for ripe fruits and vegetables. If you're unsure, it's always best to pick a little early than a little late.

When you harvest your fruits and veggies, it's all about clean removal to avoid opening a 'wound' on the plant. You should always pluck things like beans and peas from the stem joint above the pods, not right at the pod itself. Cut cucurbits from their stems at the closest joints, not directly at the top of the fruit. Tomatoes will loosen and 'fall' into your hand when they are ripe. If you do damage any of your fruit or veggies when you harvest it, be sure to eat or cook and refrigerate the damaged goods that same day.

If you're not going to be eating your fruit and vegetables fresh, you should make sure to can, freeze, dry, or otherwise preserve it as soon as you can to make sure you've not lost any nutrient content of the produce. When you freeze veggies like beans and peas, you should blanch them first to seal in the antioxidants. Don't boil them; this will leech the nutrients out of the vegetables and make them mushy when you go to thaw and reheat them. Blanching retains the nutritional value and makes the veggies useful for a variety of cooking methods, including things like soups and stir-fries.

After you've harvested and the garden is spent, it's time to prepare for winter. You want to make sure that you do everything possible to have healthy soil for the next growing season, and there are a few steps you'll need to take to put the 'bed' in raised bed. The first thing you should do is remove the remains of all annual food plants. You don't want unwanted seeds falling into the soil, leading to surprise plants next year.

Next, you should remove any annual ornamental and herb matter. Remember, you can compost any spent plant material that is free of disease. After all your annual material is removed, you'll want to cut your perennial flowers down to no more than two inches above ground level. Prune any perennial shrubs, ornamental or otherwise, and cover them with burlap, secured with twine. Trim any dead matter off of perennial ornamental vines. Once you've attended to all your plant material, it's time to take care of your soil.

Because your soil needs to last you for several seasons without being replaced, you want to add as much organic material as you can when you put your garden to bed for the off-season. Give the soil a hearty layer of compost, turning it in with a pitchfork. Stab the heck out of the soil while you're doing this- it will aerate the soil and break up any clumps that may have formed around the roots of your plants. Once you're done composting and aerating, you can either plant a cover crop, like winter rye, hairy vetch, or red clover, or you can lay a thick layer of straw (not hay!) in your beds. Now, let the beds sleep. If you have a dry winter, you can water the beds occasionally to encourage decomposition.

In the spring, you're going to want to turn all that fabulous organic material right into the soil and prep it in the same way you did when you first built the beds. Make sure that you practice good crop rotation techniques when you plant your garden again. This means moving everything one spot to the right (or clockwise) so that your heavy feeders are not in the same spot they were last year, and your legumes have a chance to replenish the soil in a new spot. Crop rotation will give your garden the opportunity to heal and regulate itself and give your plants the healthiest soil in which to grow and thrive.

One last note about raised bed gardening is that you've got to make sure to maintain the beds themselves. If you've built your beds from wood, watch for rotting or splitting, and tend to any damage immediately. You should also keep an eye on any garden structures made from masonry block, for cracks and crumbles. You don't want to have any mishaps, so it's always best to nip any structural damage in the bud. Be proactive about maintaining your beds and they will treat you to years of gardening happiness. Have fun and be creative with your design and planting, and you'll have great success at being a raised bed gardener.

PART IV

Greenhouse Gardening

Greenhouse gardening is a unique hobby that can produce stunning results for any level of gardener. Having a greenhouse means that you don't have to abide by some of the 'rules' of regular gardening because you can use a greenhouse to garden year-round and grow things that might not be considered common for your area. Although having a greenhouse can mean that you also have some additional maintenance chores, it's a rewarding undertaking for all those that attempt it.

Chapter 1: Siting and Building an Affordable Greenhouse

When you think about a greenhouse, you may think that they are too expensive to consider for your property, but there are a lot of amazing, affordable options available for would-be greenhouse gardeners today. You can build your own from a variety of materials, or you can get a pre-fabricated kit. You can also contract someone to do the construction for you if you're not comfortable with the building process. The first thing you need to do, though, is to find your site and decide on dimensions for your building. You should also check with your municipality to see if a greenhouse is considered a permanent or non-permanent structure, to determine if you need a variance or permit for the building.

Once you've determined that you can build a greenhouse and if there are any local restrictions on where you can place it, it's time to find your spot.

You want to set your greenhouse somewhere level, with plenty of sunlight, and near access to water and electricity. When you've found the perfect or largely perfect spot, measure it out and see how big a structure you can build. Keep in mind that you want something big enough to move around in, and small enough not to cost you a fortune to build. Most home greenhouses start at about 6'x9', and don't generally get too much larger than 14'x20'. A fairly standard dimension is 10'x14'.

Some materials to consider for your greenhouse structure are hardwood lumber and PVC vinyl piping if you are going to build your own greenhouse. You can use tempered glass, plexiglass, or heavy-duty plastic sheeting for the windows, and be sure to account for ventilation through vents or windows that can be opened. Building your own greenhouse can be rewarding if this is your forte, and plans are available for free or low-cost on the internet and in gardening magazines. More popular, however, are pre-fabricated kits, which are made to fit any budget. They come in all sizes and materials, so you can shop around and find what's best for you.

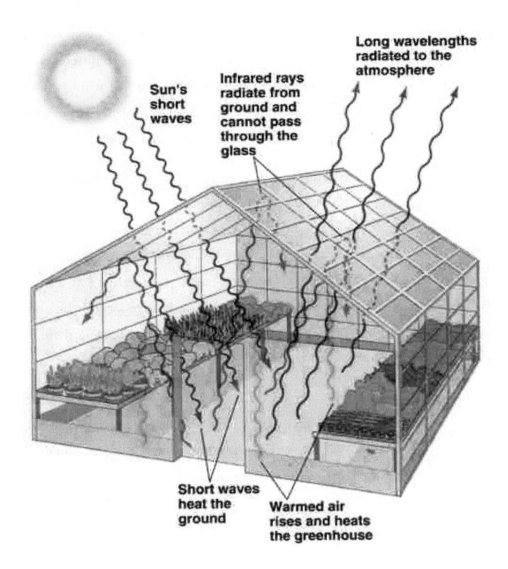

Sun's short waves

Infrared rays radiate from ground and cannot pass through the glass

Long wavelengths radiated to the atmosphere

Short waves heat the ground

Warmed air rises and heats the greenhouse

- Even without heating systems, greenhouses maintain warmer growing conditions -

Another thing to factor into the cost of erecting a greenhouse is the flooring materials. Are you going to level and pour a concrete slab, or do you think that gravel or QP (quarry process) stone is the better alternative?

This is entirely a personal decision, but when you check with your town's building or zoning officer, ask of concrete v. gravel makes a difference in whether a greenhouse is permanent or non-permanent. That might help you make your decision. Consider, too, if you'll need to spend time, money, and energy to level your property to accommodate the building.

The last expense to include when pricing out the cost of a greenhouse is water and electricity. If you need to run a supply from your house or garage to your greenhouse site, you should shop around with local electricians and plumbers to get a good value for your project. This isn't something you should attempt yourself unless you have extensive experience. If it's not too far, you can probably just run a hose and sturdy, exterior-use cord, but be aware that you'll probably have to wrap them up and bring them in every night. A dedicated underground feed is likely a better choice.

To outfit the inside of a greenhouse, let's talk briefly about the difference between a hothouse and a greenhouse. A hothouse is climate-controlled, meaning you have a heating and cooling system in place to maintain a desired temperature year-round. A greenhouse is not climate-controlled, meaning while it will extend your growing season in cooler climates, it may not still be a 12-month venture. If you're not up to investing in a full heating and cooling system, a floor model air conditioner and a space heater may be right up your alley. Consider adding an inexpensive humidifier if you live in a dry climate. Those three small appliances can usually be found cheaply or secondhand.

For greenhouse gardening, you're going to need a collection of containers, and how you choose them is entirely up to you. Some people like eclectic mismatched pots, and other like everything to match, only varying sizes to meet the needs of their plants. You'll also want some good hand tools to outfit your garden- a trowel, bulb digger, a hand rake, a pair of pruners, some utility scissors, and twine should get you set up nicely. You'll also need something to deliver your water to your plants, a sturdy watering can or a hose depending on the size of your greenhouse and your flooring. If you went with gravel, excess water would drain itself, but if you laid a concrete pad, you may want to get a long-handled squeegee to remove water from the floor and out the door.

The only other things you need for greenhouse gardening are a thermometer to keep tabs on your indoor temperature, buckets or baskets for waste and harvesting, some tool storage, and a garden journal to record your activities such as plant acquisition, major pruning, fertilizer applications, and the like. Having notes on your gardening practices helps you know what's working and what isn't, so you can make decisions for the future. If you're not into bending and twisting, you can put some tables to set your plants on and a stool to plant yourself on in the greenhouse. When you're all fitted out with tools, the last thing you'll need is a good supply of potting soil, and it's time to be a gardener!

Chapter 2: Plant Varieties for Greenhouses and Hothouses

You can grow almost anything in a greenhouse, and it's fun to decide what you'd like to cultivate. The beauty of a greenhouse, and especially a hothouse, is being able to grow things you might not be able to grow in your climate. Turning your structure into a green oasis makes it more than a place to work, it makes it a place to relax and unwind. Let's take a look at some of the plant varieties you can consider for their foliage, flowers, and food.

Philodendron- With nearly 500 varieties, you're sure to find something to love about these fast-growing vining plants. Philodendron has distinctive shiny foliage, and are easy to grow from nursery shoots in small- to medium-sized pots and hanging baskets. Philodendron will flower under warm, humid conditions, but are often kept for their foliage alone.

Alocasia- This is another plant in the same family as philodendron, and they come in a wide array of greens and patterns. Alocasia is considered to be tropical and subtropical, meaning they need warmth to thrive. They do well in greenhouses in medium pots but do require occasional re-potting as they are heavy feeders who will strip the nutrients from their soil. Purchase small seedlings from a nursery for the best results.

Geraniums- These flowering favorites do well in greenhouses year-round, and require a lot of sun and water. It's easy to buy a small flat of nursery shoots and transplant them into medium-sized pots that will provide interesting foliage all year and flowers in season. They are fragrant and come in a variety of colors.

Chrysanthemums- Outside of a greenhouse, mums are a fall staple in temperate climates. Inside a greenhouse, especially a hothouse, they can thrive all year. They come in nearly countless colors, and you can try starting them from seed or get seedlings. The delicate petals are beautiful to look at, and their faint aroma is earthy and pleasant. Mums tend to have shallow roots, so be sure to use deep pots and give them plenty of soil to avoid them 'heaving' themselves upward.

Orchids- Orchids are a classic hothouse flower, and they are popular all over the world. With their curved stalks and aromatic flowers, the cultivation of orchids can be a hobby of itself. You can try moth orchids, dendrobiums, and lady slippers to get your feet wet with this amazing species. You can encourage growth with orchid fertilizer and keep them happy by not over-watering them.

Growing Orchids

Orchids are among the most spectacular of all flowering plants. They can be planted in any container that provides adequate drainage and sufficient root ventilation.

Lighting

Most orchids require plenty of light, preferably at least six hours a day. Conversely, inadequate light prevents orchids from flowering, although they will grow.

Watering

Water orchids thoroughly, usually about once a week, and then allow them to dry slightly before watering again.

Humidity

Orchids require adequate humidity. Usually, around 60 percent or more is necessary. Use a humidifier, or set your orchids in a gravel-filled tray of water.

Roots System

Orchid roots are highly specialized organs designed to breathe and soak up water very quickly. They grow best with turbulent air circulation over their roots. The right potting mix for orchids provides plenty of drainage, air circulation or moisture depending on the needs of your particular orchids.

- Orchids are a popular plant that can become a hobby unto themselves -

Calathea- This is another great foliage plant and its varieties are often called 'prayer plants' due to the shape of the leaves, which come in a lot of different colors and patterns. These plants prefer a warmer environment but aren't too thirsty or hungry. Good soil and regular watering will keep them happy and growing. Move to larger pots to encourage larger growth, or keep them in medium pots to keep them in check, just mind that they don't get root-bound. Occasional transplanting will avoid this problem.

Nightshades- If you want to grow food in your greenhouse, it doesn't get much easier than the nightshade family, which includes tomatoes, peppers, eggplant, and potatoes. Yes! You can grow potatoes in a greenhouse if you've got a large enough container. Nightshades grow well in greenhouses because the environment keeps them from many of the insect pests that normally plague these species, and they love the warm air and sunshine. If you keep a hothouse, you can plant nightshades for food year-round and be able to enjoy fresh, juicy tomatoes in the dead of winter. Fun!

Be sure to use wide, deep pots and stake your plants so they stay upright. For best results in a greenhouse, get your nightshades from seedlings, and plant them in the container they will stay in for their whole lifecycle. You can also get seed potatoes at almost any nursery or online. Nightshades are heavy feeders, so start them out with good potting soil and give them a bump of organic plant food halfway through their growing cycle of when you see the first flowers start to appear. Don't overfeed, though. Be sure to follow package directions.

Legumes- Leguminous plants are fun to grow in a greenhouse for food, like beans and peas, and if you've got some deep containers, peanuts. The tiny, fragrant flowers on legumes are beautiful to see, as well. You can grow vining varieties of beans with stakes, or in your greenhouse corners, and they grow so quickly, you can have fresh crops year-round to eat and preserve through freezing, canning, and drying. If you're a fan of Mediterranean or Middle Eastern cuisine, you can try your hand at growing lentils and chickpeas to make your own falafel, hummus, and other dishes. Legumes grow well from either seed or seedling.

Cucurbits- This is the family of plants that includes cucumbers, melons, and squashes, and if you like them grown in a traditional garden, you'll love to grow them indoors. You can easily start cucurbits from seed or seedling, and they grow quickly as long as they have a hearty water supply. You can get compact container varieties of all your favorite cucurbits, or trellis and stake vining varieties to keep them upright and healthy. It's a really neat surprise to have a fresh watermelon on your winter holiday table!

Herbs- The hardiness and versatility of herbs make them perfect for growing in greenhouse containers. You can grow almost any herb imaginable in pots, and they provide aromatics, repel insects, and best of all, can go straight from the greenhouse to your kitchen with just a few snips. Try flowering varieties like bergamot, or discover the many cultivars of basil and oregano. The great thing about growing herbs indoors, in pots, is that the perennial species won't have the opportunity to start taking over your garden, as can sometimes happen in a traditional native soil plot. Play around with growing herbs from seeds and from nursery starts to see which you like better.

Ferns- If your greenhouse has some shade in the corners, you might want to consider growing some ferns. Ferns are a lot of fun because they come in such amazing shapes and colors. Ferns like to be warm and have nice wet soil, and they thrive in humid greenhouse environments. They don't, however, like full sun all day, so if you put them in the darkest corner of the building, they will be thrilled and reward you with terrific growth. If you want to grow some ferns, but don't have a shady corner, you can just cover the plants with a light-colored fabric during the hottest part of the day. Towels or light canvas works very well for this purpose.

These are just some of the wonderful 'starter' plants you can cultivate in a greenhouse environment. If you're considering other varieties, be sure to read the plant tags carefully before you purchase anything. Make sure that the seedlings are marked as 'compact' or 'good for containers', and take a close look at the watering and feeding requirements, as well as the spacing needs. You want to make sure you've got the right pots for your new seedlings to move into. As tempting as it can be, don't buy anything you can't provide the correct environment for.

Chapter 3: Tips and Techniques for Easy Maintenance

With your plants chosen and your greenhouse set up, you can get planting and arranging to your heart's content. The first thing you should do is set up your pots with soil, not filling them quite all the way. You want to have room to work without knocking soil all over the place. For pots where you are only placing one seedling or plant, you should make your planting space dead center, making a hole larger than the pot that the seedling came in.

You should be gentle when transplanting, giving the pot a good squeeze and, grasping the plant at the base of the stem, wiggling until the seedling comes loose. Holding it over its new container, give the roots a soft massage and placing the plant into the hole you've made. Then cover the roots and settle the soil in around the stem, pressing it lightly to hold the plant upright. For planting multiple seedlings in large containers, be sure to space them out enough so their roots have a chance to grow both down and out for stability. When your seedlings are planted, give them a good drink and let them settle into their new homes. Label your plants with their original tags or make them new ones with pertinent info.

Arrange your plants how you please in your greenhouse, but make sure not to place your containers too close to each other, as they will need airflow to stay healthy. Leave room for yourself to work and move around safely and comfortably. If you've hung work lights or have other electrical cords, make sure to tuck them away or run the cords under your tables so you don't have any tripping hazards. Safety is the name of the game when you have the potential to make a soil mess, or worse, hurt yourself!

To maintain your greenhouse plants, you should set a regular watering schedule and stick to it! Your plants will be happiest when they are well-watered. If you have any plants that need more or less frequent watering, be sure to adjust their schedule accordingly. Always water the roots of the plants, not the leaves, because wet leaves can invite infection. While weeds, pests, and pathogens are of lower concern in a greenhouse than outdoors, let's go over some basics for dealing with any issues so your plants can thrive and grow.

You can usually manually weed your pots for any intruders in a greenhouse, so just be vigilant about anything odd sprouting up in your pots. Weed seeds don't usually hide away in potting mix, but they can blow in when you've got the doors and windows open for ventilation. Take care of weeds promptly, and you won't have any undue issues. Being vigilant also helps you guard against any pests and pathogens, but the chance of invasion or infestation is never zero.

Insect pests have a way of creeping in no matter how secure your greenhouse is. Some common pests to look for are aphids and whiteflies, especially if you are growing vegetables. Take affected plants outdoors and give them a blast from the hose. The water pressure is enough to remove and drown the pests. Thrips, leaf miners, and snails and slugs also favor foliage plants, and you can treat your plants with horticultural soaps to get rid of the first two. For snails and slugs, get them drunk! Place low-sided dishes of beer near your plants at night, and in the morning, you'll have dead slugs and snails. They can't resist the lure of a good brew. Or a bad one; by all means, use up the old stuff someone left in your cooler after a BBQ last summer. Try to avoid the use of harsh insecticides in the enclosed space of your greenhouse.

Pathogens are a different issue, and you should learn to tell whether your plant has an infection or a nutrient imbalance. Your potting soil should be well-stocked with the important macronutrients (nitrogen, phosphorus, and potassium) when you first get your plants installed. As the roots take up those nutrients, heavy feeding plants can strip the nutrients from the soil. If you see signs of yellowing and curling, browning and wilting, your plant may need a food boost. You can use nutrient sticks or add compost to your containers to up the organic content.

If you see white or rusty spots on your foliage, you are likely dealing with a pathogen, not a nutrient issue. Other signs of disease include rotting roots or blossoms, leaf veins yellowing, and leaf drop. Common pathogen issues for greenhouse plants include powdery and downy mildew, leaf spot, anthracnose, and gray mold fungus. If you see signs of disease, prune away the affected tissue and dispose of it away from the greenhouse, and do not compost it. Always clean your tools with a disinfectant after cutting away diseased tissue. If you need help identifying any pests or pathogens, you should reach out to your local Cooperative Extension or Farm Bureau. They have trained staff and volunteers who can give you guidance on handling pests and disease.

Like other living beings, plants are more susceptible to issues when they are vulnerable. Keep their immune systems strong by using best gardening practices. This means good watering techniques, as well as being observant and proactive. Greenhouse plants, especially foliage plants, need a lot of TLC. You should refresh their soil with compost, or the occasional organic fertilizer, when needed. Good soil is the key to any garden but is so vital to plants in containers. It is their main source of nutrients, and you need to keep it viable to maintain plant health. Replace the soil every few years if you find that you cannot revitalize it with compost or fertilizer anymore.

You will also want to prune your foliage plants regularly to help them keep a desired shape or size, making sure to always prune at the joints to avoid 'open wounds' on the stems. You should also transplant your plants when they begin to outgrow their homes. You don't want them to become rootbound and be unable to take up nutrients. Having room to spread their roots can mean the difference between a happy plant and a distressed plant.

By being a patient, vigilant gardener, you can have healthy, thriving greenhouse plants that will reward you with beautiful foliage and flowers, as well as fresh food even in the cooler months. Using best gardening practices, asking for help when you need it, and tending to your plants' needs with gentle, knowledgeable action will give you a garden you can be proud of and want to work in every day.

Chapter 4: Crop Rotation for Year-Round Growing

If you've equipped your greenhouse to be a hothouse, you can use your space to grow year-round, which is fantastic! That means you'll be able to, if you like, do some crop rotation or succession planting, so that you don't always have the same things growing at the same time. You'll likely want to keep the foliage plants you've put so much effort into, but if you're growing vegetables, swap them out sometimes so you don't get bored with what you have.

Suitable for

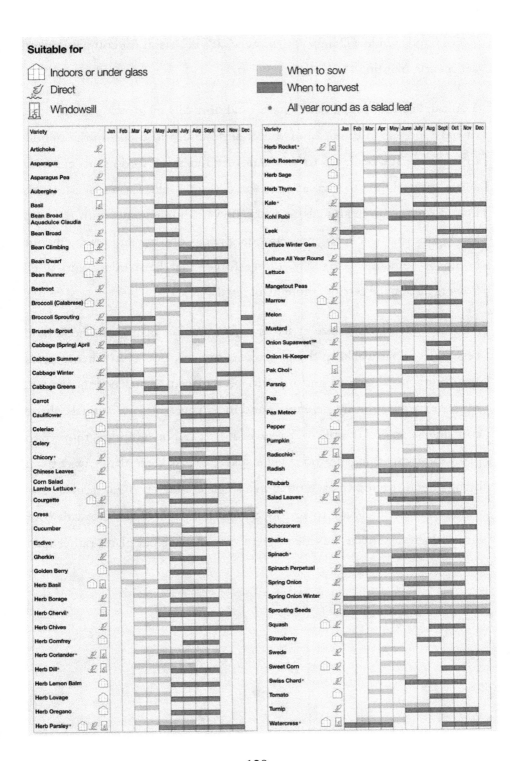

🏠 Indoors or under glass   ▨ When to sow

🐟 Direct   ▨ When to harvest

🪟 Windowsill   • All year round as a salad leaf

Variety	Jan	Feb	Mar	Apr	May	June	July	Aug	Sept	Oct	Nov	Dec
Artichoke												
Asparagus												
Asparagus Pea												
Aubergine												
Basil												
Bean Broad Aquadulce Claudia												
Bean Broad												
Bean Climbing												
Bean Dwarf												
Bean Runner												
Beetroot												
Broccoli (Calabrese)												
Broccoli Sprouting												
Brussels Sprout												
Cabbage (Spring) April												
Cabbage Summer												
Cabbage Winter												
Cabbage Greens												
Carrot												
Cauliflower												
Celeriac												
Celery												
Chicory*												
Chinese Leaves												
Corn Salad Lambs Lettuce*												
Courgette												
Cress												
Cucumber												
Endive*												
Gherkin												
Golden Berry												
Herb Basil												
Herb Borage												
Herb Chervil*												
Herb Chives												
Herb Comfrey												
Herb Coriander*												
Herb Dill*												
Herb Lemon Balm												
Herb Lovage												
Herb Oregano												
Herb Parsley*												

Variety	Jan	Feb	Mar	Apr	May	June	July	Aug	Sept	Oct	Nov	Dec
Herb Rocket*												
Herb Rosemary												
Herb Sage												
Herb Thyme												
Kale*												
Kohl Rabi												
Leek												
Lettuce Winter Gem												
Lettuce All Year Round												
Lettuce												
Mangetout Peas												
Marrow												
Melon												
Mustard												
Onion Supasweet™												
Onion Hi-Keeper												
Pak Choi*												
Parsnip												
Pea												
Pea Meteor												
Pepper												
Pumpkin												
Radicchio*												
Radish												
Rhubarb												
Salad Leaves*												
Sorrel*												
Schorzonera												
Shallots												
Spinach*												
Spinach Perpetual												
Spring Onion												
Spring Onion Winter												
Sprouting Seeds												
Squash												
Strawberry												
Swede												
Sweet Corn												
Swiss Chard*												
Tomato												
Turnip												
Watercress*												

- This handy guide will help you know what's in season for companion and succession planting -

You can keep in season with what would normally be growing at the time, or have melons in the dead of winter and butternut squash in the middle of summer. It's really up to you. Another fun thing to do is to cultivate some spring bulbs to give as gifts for occasions like Easter or Mother's Day. Planting some annuals to make flower arrangements with is also a lovely idea that will keep your gardening juices flowing and brighten your home or someone else's day. Don't forget that herb mixes and dried flowers also make terrific, thoughtful gifts!

Another way to maximize space is to companion plant your herbs and vegetables. That will keep things growing in every pot, even when veggies are done with their run and need to be replaced or succession planted. Because most herbs are perennials and most vegetables are annuals, those containers can pull double duty year-round. It can be tempting, though, to plant too many things in too small a space. Try to keep plants away from being directly on top of each other in a single container. A good rule is that if it seems like it's going to be too cramped, it probably is. Go with your gut, and always err on the side of giving more space per plant, rather than less.

Chapter 5: Structural Upkeep for Long-term Use

Greenhouse gardening is a big commitment, because not only do you have to take care of the plants inside, you also need to take care of the structure itself. Take care to check your building for any structural damage, especially after storms. Replace any cracked glass or plexiglass as soon as you can, and if you've got a plastic greenhouse, look for any tears in the sheeting. By taking care of small issues before they become big ones, you'll save yourself lots of time, money, and frustration.

If your greenhouse is built with a wooden frame, be sure to keep it painted or water-sealed for extra protection from the elements. For structures made of PVC piping, it can be a good idea to use caulk or another sealant at the joints to make sure that moisture stays out of the materials. Keep an eye on the floors and doors of your building, too. If you've got a concrete slab, seal up any cracks to prevent further damage. Gravel floors should be refreshed every so often when you can afford to do so. Check that your door(s) close snugly and fix any loose hinges.

For gardeners that live in areas that get snow or ice, it's important to have a system in place to keep that winter weather from damaging your greenhouse. Get a good long-handled roof snow brush, and promptly remove as much snow as you can, especially if it's wet heavy snow that can be common in most temperate climes. A little preventative maintenance goes a long way! Make sure you occasionally get on a ladder and check out the ceiling/roof of your greenhouse, too. You don't want to be surprised by any falling panels or leaky tears in the roof! It's all about maintaining safety.

Humidity Too Low	Humidity Too High
Wilting	Soft growth
Stunted plants	Increased foliar disease
Smaller leaf size	Nutrient deficiencies
Dry tip burn	Increased root disease
Leaf curl	Oedema
Increased infestation of spider mites	Edge burn (guttation)

- Don't forget to mind your humidity levels and keep your greenhouse well-vented all year long!-

By keeping your plants inside happy and healthy and your structure sound and sturdy, you are well on your way to being an experienced greenhouse gardener. Keep the temperature steady, keep your plants watered and fed, and keep the building in good condition, and you will have a garden and greenhouse to be proud of for many, many years. Have fun!

One of the greatest things, or perhaps, THE greatest thing about being a gardener is that it allows you a lot of freedom to explore and express your interests. Hobby gardeners wear a lot of hats- they are manual laborers, researchers, scientists, chefs, florists, readers, writers, and naturalists. Along with those roles comes the inevitable. You cannot help yourself but learn, even if you learn by failing. The wonderful thing about plants is that you can take a seed, nurture it, feed and water it, and watch it live its entire life cycle under your care, and then! Just when you are mourning the loss of a particularly abundant tomato plant or the dying off of your annual flowers, you remember, you get to do this again next year. You get to be a part of the renewal of spring. It's an amazing feeling. Just the sheer act of putting your hands in the soil can be calming; it awakens your senses and lowers your stress levels.

Use your off-seasons wisely. Read up on the plant species and varieties that you want to discover more about. Everyone who gardens eventually finds their niche. Some are obsessed with vegetables, some with soil health, and some devote their gardening efforts to growing stunning floral displays. You'll find your niche, too. Take the time to explore the many fascinating facets of gardening. It's fun to learn about new plants and catch up on the latest news in botany and the life sciences.

- Put your journal to good use in the off-season with notes and new designs
-

Another awesome byproduct of gardening is how much closer you will feel to your environment. When you spend time outdoors or in a greenhouse with clear walls, you can see and hear what's happening around you. There is birdsong and the buzzing of insects, and on hot days, you can almost hear your plants speaking to you as they stand tall in the sun and wave in the summer breeze. It's magical. Let it both transport you and ground you, and you'll wonder how you ever lived without your garden.

Gardening also teaches you to be creative in other parts of your life. You can learn to cook with new ingredients, or take up canning and food preservation. You can practice making flower arrangements, or drying flowers for crafts. Gardening begets other hobbies, and it's easy to branch out into beautiful artwork and crafts to share with your family and friends.

You can also leave your plants in the garden and capture them in other ways, like photography or painting. Let your garden be your muse in all things.

The point is, learning how to grow a basic garden is only the beginning for you. You can use the planning and execution skills learned in gardening to expand your horizons into so many other things. So be curious. Ask why certain pests attack certain plants. Figure out how to stop it from happening. Watch what birds come to your garden at particular times of the year, and wonder if they are beneficial. Be a voracious researcher. You'll soon discover that the more you know, the more you will want to know. It's empowering in a way few hobbies can be.

- Flex your gardening muscles in the winter with indoor herbs! -

Gardening can also be frustrating, but take heart. For every step back, there will be more steps forward. Sometimes, we can do everything correctly and still fail! Weather can be a harsh mistress, and invasive insects can cause harm before anyone even knows they exist. Be stronger than the setbacks and don't get discouraged. Even the best plant scientists in the world lose crops sometimes. And sometimes, they are just winging things, too. So have fun. Read. Take notes. Sit in your garden and watch the bumblebees do their pollination thing. Most of all, take time to smell the flowers. The gardening world is your oyster, crack it open and find all the pearls!

PART V

Sirtfood Diet

The sirtfood diet is one of the latest diet patterns that has garnered quite the attention. The idea was brought to the market by two nutritionists Glen Matten and Aidan Goggins. The main idea of the diet revolves around sirtuins, which are basically a group of 7 proteins that are responsible for the functioning and regulation of lifespan, inflammation, and metabolism (Sergiy Libert, 2013).

Chapter 1: Health Benefits of the Diet

The benefits are vast. This includes loss in weight, better skin quality, gain in muscle mass in the areas that are very much required, increased metabolic rate, feeling of fullness without having to eat much (this is the power of the foods actually), suppressing the appetite, and leading a better and confident life. This specifically includes an increase in the memory, supporting the body to control blood sugar and blood cholesterol level in a much-advanced way, and wiping out the damage caused by the free radicals and thus preventing them from having adverse impacts on the cells that might lead to other diseases like cancer.

The consumption of these foods, along with the drinks, has a number of observational shreds of evidence that link the sirtfoods with the reducing hazards of several chronic diseases. This diet is notably suited as an anti-aging scheme. Sirtfoods have the ability to satiate the appetite in a natural way and increase the functioning of the muscle. These two points are enough to find a solution that can ultimately help us to achieve a healthy weight. In addition to this, the health-improving impact of these compounds is powerful in comparison to the drugs that are prescribed in order to prevent several chronic diseases like that of diabetes, heart problems, Alzheimer's, etc.

A pilot study was conducted on a total of 39 participants. At the end of the first week, the participants had an increase in muscle mass and also lost 7 pounds on average. Research has proven that in this initial week, the weight loss that is witnessed is mostly from water, glycogen, and muscle, and only one-third of it is from fat (Manfred J. Müller, 2016). The major sirtfoods include red wine, kale, soy, strawberries, matcha green tea, extra virgin olive oil, walnuts, buckwheat, capers, lovage, coffee, dark chocolate, Medjool dates, turmeric, red chicory, parsley, onions, arugula, and blueberries (Kathrin Pallauf, 2013).

Chapter 2: Sirtfood Juice Recipes

Green Juice

Total Prep & Cooking Time: Five minutes

Yields: 1 serving

Nutrition Facts: Calories: 182.3 | Carbs: 42.9g | Protein: 6g | Fat: 1.5g | Fiber: 12.7g

Ingredients:

- Half a green apple
- Two sticks of celery
- Five grams of parsley
- Thirty grams of rocket
- Seventy-five grams of kale
- Half a teaspoon of matcha green tea
- Juice of half a lemon
- One cm of ginger

Method:

1. Juice the kale, rocket, celery sticks, green apple, and parsley in a juicer.

2. Add the lemon juice into the green juice by squeezing it with your hand.

3. Take a glass and pour a little amount of the green juice into it. Add the matcha green tea and stir it in. Then, pour the remaining green juice into the glass and stir to combine everything properly.

4. You can choose to save it for later or drink it straight away.

Blueberry Kale Smoothie

Total Prep & Cooking Time: Five minutes

Yields: 1 serving

Nutrition Facts: Calories: 240 | Carbs: 37.9g | Protein: 17.2g | Fat: 3.6g | Fiber: 7g

Ingredients:

- Half a cup each of
  - Plain low-fat yogurt
  - Blueberries (frozen or fresh)
  - Kale, chopped
- Half a banana
- Half a teaspoon of cinnamon powder
- One tablespoon of flaxseed meal
- One scoop of protein powder
- Half a cup of water (optional)
- Two handfuls of ice (you can add more if you like)

Method:

1. Take a high-speed blender and add all the ingredients in it.

2. Blend everything together until you get a smooth puree.

3. Pour the blueberry kale smoothie in a glass and serve cold.

Tropical Kale Smoothie

Total Prep & Cooking Time: 10 minutes

Yields: 2 servings

Nutrition Facts: Calories: 187 | Carbs: 46.8g | Protein: 3.5g | Fat: 0.5g | Fiber: 4.7g

Ingredients:

- Half a cup to one cup of orange juice (about 120 ml to 240 ml)
- One banana, chopped (use frozen banana, is possible)
- Two cups of pineapple (about 330 grams), chopped (use frozen pineapple if possible)
- One and a half cups of kale (around 90 grams), chopped

Method:

1. Add the chopped bananas, pineapple, kale, and orange juice into a blender and blend everything together until you get a smooth puree.

2. You can add more orange juice if you need to attain a smoothie consistency. The amount of frozen fruit used directly affects the consistency of the smoothie.

3. Pour the smoothie equally into two glasses and serve cold.

Strawberry Oatmeal Smoothie

Total Prep & Cooking Time: 5 minutes

Yields: 2 servings

Nutrition Facts: Calories: 236.1 | Carbs: 44.9g | Protein: 7.6g | Fat: 3.7g | Fiber: 5.9g

Ingredients:

- Half a tsp. of vanilla extract
- Fourteen frozen strawberries
- One banana (cut into chunks)
- Half a cup of rolled oats
- One cup of soy milk
- One and a half tsps. of white sugar

Method:

1. Take a blender. Add the strawberries, banana, oats, and soy milk.

2. Then add sugar and vanilla extract.

3. Blend until the texture becomes smooth.

4. Then pour it into a glass and serve.

Chapter 3: Main Course Recipes for Sirtfood Diet

Green Juice Salad
Total Prep & Cooking Time: Ten minutes

Yields: 1 serving

Nutrition Facts: Calories: 199 | Carbs: 27g | Protein: 10g | Fat: 8.2g | Fiber: 9.2g

Ingredients:

- Six walnuts, halved
- Half of a green apple, sliced
- Two sticks of celery, sliced
- One tablespoon each of
  o Parsley
  o Olive oil
- One handful of rocket
- Two handfuls of kale, sliced
- One cm of ginger, grated
- Juice of half a lemon
- Salt and pepper to taste

Method:

1. To make the dressing, add the olive oil, ginger, lemon juice, salt, and pepper in a jam jar. Shake the jar to combine everything together.

2. Keep the sliced kale in a large bowl and add the dressing over it. Massage the dressing for about a minute to mix it with the kale properly.

3. Lastly, add the remaining ingredients (walnuts, sliced green apple, celery sticks, parsley, and rocket) into the bowl and combine everything thoroughly.

King Prawns and Buckwheat Noodles

Total Prep & Cooking Time: Twenty minutes

Yields: 4 servings

Nutrition Facts: Calories: 496 | Carbs: 53.2g | Protein: 22.2g | Fat: 17.6g | Fiber: 4.8g

Ingredients:

- 600 grams of king prawn
- 300 grams of soba or buckwheat noodles (using 100 percent buckwheat is recommended)
- One bird's eye chili, membranes, and seeds eliminated and finely chopped (and more according to taste)
- Three cloves of garlic, finely chopped or grated
- Three cm of ginger, grated
- 100 grams of green beans, chopped
- 100 grams of kale, roughly chopped
- Two celery sticks, sliced
- One red onion, thinly sliced
- Two tablespoons each of
  - Parsley, finely chopped (or lovage, if you have it)
  - Soy sauce or tamari (and extra for serving)
  - Extra virgin olive oil

Method:

1. Boil the buckwheat noodles for three to five minutes or until they are cooked according to your liking. Drain the water and then rinse the noodles in cold water. Drizzle some olive oil on the top and mix it with the noodles. Keep this mixture aside.

2. Prepare the remaining ingredients while the noodles are boiling.

3. Place a large frying pan or a wok over low heat and add a little olive oil into it. Then add the celery and red onions and fry them for about three minutes so that they get soft.

4. Then add the green beans and kale and increase the heat to medium-high. Fry them for about three minutes.

5. Decrease the heat again and then add the prawns, chili, ginger, and garlic into the pan. Fry for another two to three minutes so that the prawns get hot all the way through.

6. Lastly, add in the buckwheat noodles, soy sauce/tamari, and cook it for another minute so that the noodles get warm again.

7. Sprinkle some chopped parsley on the top as a garnish and serve hot.

Red Onion Dhal and Buckwheat

Total Prep & Cooking Time: Thirty minutes

Yields: 4 servings

Nutrition Facts: Calories: 154 | Carbs: 9g | Protein: 19g | Fat: 2g | Fiber: 12g

Ingredients:

- 160 grams of buckwheat or brown rice
- 100 grams of kale (spinach would also be a good alternative)
- 200 ml of water
- 400 ml of coconut milk
- 160 grams of red lentils
- Two teaspoons each of
  - Garam masala
  - Turmeric
- One bird's eye chili, deseeded and finely chopped (plus more if you want it extra hot)
- Two cms of ginger, grated
- Three cloves of garlic, crushed or grated
- One red onion (small), sliced
- One tablespoon of olive oil

Method:

1. Take a large, deep saucepan and add the olive oil in it. Add the sliced onion and cook it on low heat with the lid closed for about five minutes so that they get softened.

2. Add the chili, ginger, and garlic and cook it for another minute.

3. Add a splash of water along with the garam masala and turmeric and cook for another minute.

4. Next add the coconut milk, red lentils along with 200 ml of water. You can do this by filling the can of coconut milk halfway with water and adding it into the saucepan.

5. Combine everything together properly and let it cook over low heat for about twenty minutes. Keep the lid on and keep stirring occasionally. If the dhal starts to stick to the pan, add a little more water to it.

6. Add the kale after twenty minutes and stir properly and put the lid back on. Let it cook for another five minutes. (If you're using spinach instead, cook for an additional one to two minutes)

7. Add the buckwheat in a medium-sized saucepan about fifteen minutes before the curry is cooked.

8. Add lots of boiling water into the buckwheat and boil the water again—Cook for about ten minutes. If you prefer softer buckwheat, you can cook it for a little longer.

9. Drain the buckwheat using a sieve and serve along with the dhal.

Chicken Curry

Total Prep & Cooking Time: 45 minutes

Yields: 4 servings

Nutrition Facts: Calories: 243 | Carbs: 7.5g | Protein: 28g | Fat: 11g | Fiber: 1.5g

Ingredients:

- 200 grams of buckwheat (you can also use basmati rice or brown rice)
- One 400ml tin of coconut milk
- Eight skinless and boneless chicken thighs, sliced into bite-sized chunks (you can also use four chicken breasts)
- One tablespoon of olive oil
- Six cardamom pods (optional)
- One cinnamon stick (optional)
- Two teaspoons each of
  - Ground turmeric
  - Ground cumin
  - Garam masala
- Two cm. of fresh ginger, peeled and coarsely chopped
- Three cloves of garlic, roughly chopped
- One red onion, roughly chopped
- Two tablespoons of freshly chopped coriander (and more for garnishing)

Method:

1. Add the ginger, garlic, and onions in a food processor and blitz to get a paste. You can also use a hand blender to make the paste. If you have neither, just finely chop the three ingredients and continue the following steps.

2. Add the turmeric powder, cumin, and garam masala into the paste and combine them together. Keep the paste aside.

3. Take a wide, deep pan (preferably a non-stick pan) and add one tablespoon of olive oil into it. Heat it over high heat for about a minute and then add the pieces of boneless chicken thighs. Increase the heat and stir-fry the chicken thighs for about two minutes. Then, reduce the heat and add the curry paste. Let the chicken cook in the curry paste for about three minutes and then pour half of the coconut milk (about 200ml) into it. You can also add the cardamom and cinnamon if you're using them.

4. Let it boil for some time and then reduce the heat and let it simmer for thirty minutes. The curry sauce will get thick and delicious.

5. You can add a splash of coconut milk if your curry sauce begins to get dry. You might not need to add extra coconut milk at all, but you can add it if you want a slightly more saucy curry.

6. Prepare your side dishes and other accompaniments (buckwheat or rice) while the curry is cooking.

7. Add the chopped coriander as a garnish when the curry is ready and serve immediately with the buckwheat or rice.

Chickpea Stew With Baked Potatoes

Total Prep & Cooking Time: One hour and ten minutes

Yields: 4 to 6 servings

Nutrition Facts: Calories: 348.3 | Carbs: 41.2g | Protein: 7.2g | Fat: 16.5g | Fiber: 5.3g

Ingredients:

- Two yellow peppers, chopped into bite-sized pieces (you can also use other colored bell peppers)
- Two 400-grams tins each of
  o Chickpeas (you can also use kidney beans) (don't drain the water if you prefer including it)
  o Chopped tomatoes
- Two cm. of ginger, grated
- Four cloves of garlic, crushed or grated
- Two red onions, finely chopped
- Four to six potatoes, prickled all over
- Two tablespoons each of
  o Turmeric
  o Cumin seeds
  o Olive oil
  o Unsweetened cocoa powder (or cacao, if you want)
  o Parsley (and extra for garnishing)
- Half a teaspoon to two teaspoons of chili flakes (you can add according to how hot you like things)
- A splash of water
- Side salad (optional)
- Salt and pepper according to your taste (optional)

Method:

1. Preheat your oven to 200 degrees Celsius.

2. In the meantime, prepare all the other ingredients.

3. Place your baking potatoes in the oven when it gets hot enough and allow it to cook for an hour so that they are cooked according to your preference. You can also use your regular method to bake the potatoes if it's different from this method.

4. When the potatoes are cooking in the oven, place a large wide saucepan over low heat and add the olive oil along with the chopped red onion into it. Keep the lid on and let the onions cook for five minutes. The onions should turn soft but shouldn't turn brown.

5. Take the lid off and add the chili, cumin, ginger, and garlic into the saucepan. Let it cook on low heat for another minute and then add the turmeric along with a tiny splash of water and cook it for a further minute. Make sure that the pan does not get too dry.

6. Then, add in the yellow pepper, canned chickpeas (along with the chickpea liquid), cacao or cocoa powder, and chopped tomatoes. Bring the mixture to a boil and then let it simmer on low heat for about forty-five minutes so that the sauce gets thick and unctuous (make sure that it doesn't burn). The stew and the potatoes should complete cooking at roughly the same time.

7. Finally, add some salt and pepper as per your taste along with the parsley and stir them in the stew.

8. You can add the stew on top of the baked potatoes and serve. You can also serve the stew with a simple side salad.

Blueberry Pancakes

Total Prep & Cooking Time: 25 minutes

Yields: 2 servings

Nutrition Facts: Calories: 84 | Carbs: 11g | Protein: 2.3g | Fat: 3.5g | Fiber: 0g

Ingredients:

- 225 grams of blueberries
- 150 grams of rolled oats
- Six eggs
- Six bananas
- One-fourth of a teaspoon of salt
- Two teaspoons of baking powder

Method:

1. Add the rolled oats in a high-speed blender and pulse it for about a minute or so to get the oat flour. Before adding the oats to the blender, make sure that it is very dry. Otherwise, your oat flour will turn soggy.

2. Then, add the eggs and bananas along with the salt and baking soda into the blender and blend them together for another two minutes until you get a smooth batter.

3. Take a large bowl and transfer the mixture into it. Then add the blueberries and fold them into the mixture. Let it rest for about ten minutes to allow the baking powder to activate.

4. To make the pancakes, place a frying pan on medium-high heat and add a dollop of butter into it. The butter will help to make your pancakes really crispy and delicious.

5. Add a few spoonfuls of the blueberry pancake batter into the frying pan and cook it until the bottom side turns golden. Once the bottom turns golden, toss the pancake and fry the other side.

6. Serve them hot and enjoy.

Sirtfood Bites

Total Prep & Cooking Time: 1 hour + 15 minutes

Yields: 15-20 bites

Nutrition Facts: Calories: 58.1 | Carbs: 10.1g | Protein: 0.9g | Fat: 2.3g | Fiber: 1.2g

Ingredients:

- One tablespoon each of
  - Extra virgin olive oil
  - Ground turmeric
  - Cocoa powder
- Nine ounces of Medjool dates, pitted (about 250 grams)
- One ounce (about thirty grams) of dark chocolate (85% cocoa solids), break them into pieces (you can also use one-fourth of a cup of cocoa nibs)
- One teaspoon of vanilla extract (you can also take the scraped seeds of one vanilla pod)
- One cup of walnuts (about 120 grams)
- One to two tablespoons of water

Method:

1. Add the chocolate and walnuts in a food processor and blitz them until you get a fine powder.

2. Add the Medjool dates, cocoa powder, ground turmeric, extra-virgin olive oil, and vanilla extract into the food processor and blend them together until the mixture forms a ball. Depending on the consistency of the mixture, you can choose to add or skip the water. Make sure that the mixture is not too sticky.

3. Make bite-sized balls from the mixture using your hands and keep them in the refrigerator in an airtight container. Refrigerate them for at least an hour before consuming them.

4. To get a finish of your liking, you can roll the balls in some more dried coconut or cocoa. You can store the balls in the refrigerator for up to a week.

Flank Steak With Broccoli Cauliflower Gratin

Total Prep & Cooking Time: 55 minutes

Yields: 4 servings

Nutrition Facts: Calories: 839 | Carbs: 8g | Protein: 43g | Fat: 70g | Fiber: 3g

Ingredients:

- Two tablespoons of olive oil
- Twenty ounces of flank steak
- One-fourth teaspoon salt
- Four ounces of divided shredded cheese
- Half cup of heavy whipping cream
- Eight ounces of cauliflower
- Eight ounces of broccoli
- Salt and pepper

For the pepper sauce,

- One tablespoon soy sauce
- One and a half cups of heavy whipping cream
- Half teaspoon ground black pepper

For the garnishing,

- Two tablespoons of freshly chopped parsley

Method:

1. At first, you have to preheat your oven to four hundred degrees Fahrenheit. Then you need to apply butter on a baking dish (eight by eight inches).

2. Then you have to clean and then trim the cauliflower and broccoli. Then you need to cut them into florets, and their stem needs to be sliced.

3. Then you have to boil the broccoli and cauliflower for about five minutes in salted water.

4. After boiling, you need to drain out all the water and keep the vegetables aside. Then you have to take a saucepan over medium heat and add half portion of the shredded cheese, heavy cream, and salt. Then you need to whisk them together until the cheese gets melted. Then you have to add the cauliflower and the broccoli and mix them in.

5. Place the cauliflower and broccoli mixture in a baking dish. Then you have to take the rest half portion of the cheese and add—Bake for about twenty minutes in the oven.

6. Season with salt and pepper on both sides of the meat.

7. Then you have to take a large frying pan over medium-high heat and fry the meat for about four to five minutes on each side.

8. After that, take a cutting board and place the meat on it. Then you have to leave the meat for about ten to fifteen minutes before you start to slice it.

9. Take the frying pan, and in it, you need to pour soy sauce, cream, and pepper. Then you have to bring it to a boil and allow the sauce to simmer until the sauce becomes creamy in texture. Then you need to taste it and then season it with some more salt and pepper according to your taste.

Kale Celery Salad

Total Prep & Cooking Time: 15 minutes

Yields: 4 servings

Nutrition Facts: 196 | Carbs: 20g | Protein: 5.7g | Fat: 11.5g | Fiber: 4.8g

Ingredients:

- Half a cup of crumbled feta cheese
- Half a cup of chopped and toasted walnuts
- One wedge lemon
- One red apple, crisp
- Two celery stalks
- Eight dates, pitted dried
- Four cups of washed and dried baby kale (stemmed)

For the dressing,

- Three tbsps. olive oil
- One tsp. maple syrup (or you can use any other sweetener as per your preference)
- Four tsps. balsamic vinegar
- Freshly ground salt and black pepper

Method:

1. At first, you have to take a platter or a wide serving bowl. Then you need to place the baby kale in it.

2. Cut the dates into very thin slices, lengthwise. Then you need to place it in another small bowl.

3. After that, you have to peel the celery and then cut them into halves, lengthwise.

4. Then you need to take your knife, hold it in a diagonal angle, and then cut the celery into thin pieces (approximately one to two inches each). Add these pieces to the dates.

5. Then you have to cut the sides off the apple. You need to cut very thin slices from those pieces.

6. Over the apple slices, you need to put some lemon juice to prevent them from browning.

7. For preparing the dressing, you have to take a small bowl, add maple syrup, olive oil, and vinegar. Then you need to whisk them together.

8. Once done, you have to season with freshly ground pepper and two pinches of salt.

9. Before serving, you need to take most of the dressing and pour it over the salad. Then you have to toss nicely so that they get combined. Then you need to pour the rest of the portion of the dressing over the dates and celery.

10. On the top, you have to add the date mixture, feta cheese, apple slices, and walnuts.

Buckwheat Stir Fry

Total Prep & Cooking Time: 28 minutes

Yields: 8 servings

Nutrition Facts: Calories: 258 | Carbs: 35.1g | Protein: 6.8g | Fat: 11.9g | Fiber: 2g

Ingredients:

For the buckwheat,

- Three cups of water
- One and a half cups of uncooked roasted buckwheat groats
- Pinch of salt

For the stir fry,

- Half a cup of finely chopped basil
- Half a cup of finely chopped parsley
- One teaspoon salt
- Four tablespoons of divided red palm oil or coconut oil
- Two cups of drained and chopped marinated artichoke hearts
- Four large bell peppers (sliced into strips)
- Four large minced cloves of garlic
- One bunch of finely chopped kale (ribs removed)

Method:

For making the buckwheat,

1. In a medium-sized pot, pour the buckwheat. Then rinse with cold water and drain the water. Repeat this process for about two to three times.

2. Then add three cups of water to it and also add a pinch of salt. Cover the pot and bring it to a boil.

3. Reduce the heat to low and then cook for about fifteen minutes. Keep the lid on and remove the pot from the heat.

4. Leave it for three minutes and then fluff with a fork.

For making the stir fry,

1. At first, you have to take a ceramic non-stick wok and preheat over medium heat. Then you need to add one tablespoon of oil and coat it. Then you have to add garlic and then sauté for about ten seconds. Then you need to add kale and then add one-fourth teaspoon of salt. Then you need to sauté it accompanied by occasional stirring, until it shrinks in half. Then you have to transfer it to a medium-sized bowl.

2. Then again return to the wok, turn the heat on high, and pour one tablespoon of oil. You need to add one-fourth teaspoon salt and pepper. Then you have to sauté it until it turns golden brown in color. Once done, you need to place it in the bowl containing kale.

3. Then you have to reduce the heat to low, and you need to add two tablespoons of oil. Add the cooked buckwheat and stir it nicely so that it gets coated in the oil. Then after turning off the heat, you need to add the kale and peppers, basil, parsley, artichoke hearts, and half teaspoon salt. Gently stir and serve it hot.

Kale Omelet

Total Prep & Cooking Time: 10 minutes

Yields: 1 serving

Nutrition Facts: Calories: 339 | Carbs: 8.6g | Protein: 15g | Fat: 28.1g | Fiber: 4.4g

Ingredients:

- One-fourth sliced avocado
- Pinch of red pepper (crushed)
- One tsp. sunflower seeds (unsalted)
- One tbsp. of freshly chopped cilantro
- One tbsp. lime juice
- One cup of chopped kale
- Two tsps. of extra-virgin olive oil
- One tsp. of low-fat milk
- Two eggs
- Salt

Method:

1. At first, take a small bowl and pour milk. Then you have to add the eggs and salt to it. Beat the mixture thoroughly. Then take a small non-stick skillet over medium heat, and add one tsp. of oil and heat it. Then add the egg mixture and cook for about one to two minutes, until the time you notice that the center is still a bit runny, but the bottom has become set. Then you need to flip the omelet and cook the other side for another thirty seconds until it is set too. One done, transfer the omelet to a plate.

2. Toss the kale with one tsp. of oil, sunflower seeds, cilantro, lime juice, salt, and crushed red pepper in another bowl. Then return to the omelet on the plate and top it off with avocado and the kale salad.

Tuna Rocket Salad

Total Prep & Cooking Time: 20 minutes

Yields: 4 servings

Nutrition Facts: Calories: 321 | Carbs: 20g | Protein: 33g | Fat: 12g | Fiber: 9.5g

Ingredients:

- Twelve leaves of basil (fresh)
- Two bunches of washed and dried rocket (trimmed)
- One and a half tbsps. of olive oil
- Freshly ground black pepper and salt
- Sixty grams of kalamata olives cut into halves, lengthwise (drained pitted)
- One thinly sliced and halved red onion
- Two coarsely chopped ripe tomatoes
- Four hundred grams of rinsed and drained cannellini beans
- Four hundred grams of drained tuna
- 2 cm cubes of one multigrain bread roll

Method:

1. At first, you need to preheat your oven to 200 degrees Celsius.

2. After that, take a baking tray and line it with a foil.

3. Then you have to spread the cubes of bread over the baking tray evenly.

4. Put the baking tray inside the oven and cook it for about ten minutes until it turns golden in color.

5. In the meantime, you have to take a large bowl and add the olives, onions, tomatoes, cannellini beans, and tuna. Then you need to season it with pepper and salt. Add some oil and then toss for smooth combining.

6. Your next step is to add the basil leaves, croutons, and the rocket. Then you need to toss gently to combine. After that, you can divide the salad into the serving bowls and serve.

Turmeric Baked Salmon

Total Prep & Cooking Time: 30 minutes

Yields: 4 servings

Nutrition Facts: Calories: 448 | Carbs: 2g | Protein: 34g | Fat: 33g | Fiber: 0.2g

Ingredients:

- One ripe yellow lemon
- Half a teaspoon of salt
- One teaspoon turmeric
- One tablespoon of dried thyme
- Half a cup of frozen, salted butter (you may require some more for greasing the pan)
- Four fresh one and a half inches thick salmon fillets (skin-on)

Method:

1. At first, you need to preheat your oven to 400 degrees Fahrenheit. Then with a thin layer of butter, you need to grease the bottom of the baking sheet. Rinse the salmon fillets and pat them dry. Then you have to place the salmon fillets on the buttered baking dish keeping the skin side down.

2. Take the lemons and cut them into four round slices. Remove the seeds and then cut each slice into two halves. Then you will have eight pieces.

3. Take a small dish and combine turmeric, dried thyme, and salt. Then you need to mix them well until they are nicely combined. On the top of the salmon fillets, you need to evenly sprinkle the spice mixture.

4. Place two lemon slices over each salmon fillet.

5. After that, you need to grate the cold butter on the top of the salmon fillets evenly. Allow the butter to meltdown and form a delicious sauce.

6. Then you have to cover the pan with parchment or aluminum foil. Put it inside the oven and cook for about fifteen to twenty minutes according to your desire. The cooking time is dependent on the thickness of the salmon fillets. You can check whether it is done or not by cutting into the center.

7. Once done, remove it from the oven and then uncover it. The butter sauce needs to be spooned over from the tray.

8. Top it off with fresh mint and serve.

Chapter 4: One-Week Meal Plan

Day 1

8 AM – Green Juice

12 PM - Blueberry Kale Smoothie

4 PM – Tropical Kale Smoothie

8 PM – Turmeric Baked Salmon

Day 2

8 AM – Tropical Kale Smoothie

12 PM – Green Juice

4 PM – Strawberry Oatmeal Smoothie

8 PM – King Prawns and Buckwheat Noodles

Day 3

8 AM – Strawberry Oatmeal Smoothie

12 PM – Tropical Kale Smoothie

4 PM – Green Juice

8 PM – Buckwheat Stir Fry

Day 4

8 AM – Blueberry Kale Smoothie

12 PM – Green Juice

4 PM – Green Juice Salad

8 PM – Tuna Rocket Salad

Day 5

8 AM – Green Juice

12 PM – Tropical Kale Smoothie

4 PM – Sirtfood Bites

8 PM – Chicken Curry

Day 6

8 AM – Strawberry Oatmeal Smoothie

12 PM – Green Juice

4 PM – Kale Celery Salad

8 PM – Flank Steak with Broccoli Cauliflower Gratin

Day 7

8 AM – Tropical Kale Smoothie

12 PM – Blueberry Kale Smoothie

4 PM – Kale Omelet

8 PM – Chickpea Stew with Baked Potatoes

PART VI

Reset Diet

In this chapter, we are going to study the details of the reset diet and what recipes you can make.

Chapter 1: How to Reset Your Body?

Created by a celebrity trainer, Harley Pasternak, the body reset diet is a famous fifteen-day eating pattern that aims to jump-start weight loss. According to Pasternak, if you experience rapid loss in weight early in a diet, you will feel more motivated to stick to that diet plan. This theory is even supported by a few scientific studies (Alice A Gibson, 2017).

The body reset diet claims to help in weight loss with light exercise and low-calorie diet plans for fifteen days. The diet is divided into 3 phases of five days each. Each phase had a particular pattern of diet and exercise routine. You need to consume food five times every day, starting from the first phase, which mostly consists of smoothies and progressing to more solid foods in the second and third phases.

The three phases of the body reset diet are:

- **Phase One** – During this stage, you are required to consume only two snacks every day and drink smoothies for breakfast, lunch, and dinner. In the case of exercise, you have to walk at least ten thousand steps per day.

- **Phase Two** – During this phase, you can eat two snacks each day, consume solid food only once, and have to replace any two meals of the day with smoothies. In case of exercise, apart from walking ten thousand steps every day, on three of the days, you also have to finish five minutes of resistance training with the help of four separate exercises.

- **Phase Three** – You can consume two snacks every day, but you have to eat two low-calorie meals and replace one of your meals with a smoothie. For exercise, you are required to walk ten thousand steps. Apart from that, you also have to finish five minutes of resistance training with the help of four separate exercises each day.

After you have finished the standard fifteen-day diet requirements, you have to keep following the meal plan you followed in the third phase. However, during this time, you are allowed to have two "free meals" twice a week in which you can consume anything you want. These "free meals" are meant as a reward so that you can avoid feeling deprived. According to Pasternak, depriving yourself of a particular food continuously can result in binge eating (Nawal Alajmi, 2016).

There is no official endpoint of the diet after the first fifteen days for losing and maintaining weight. Pasternak suggests that the habits and routines formed over fifteen days should be maintained for a lifetime.

Chapter 2: Science Behind Metabolism Reset

Several people take on a "cleanse" or "detox" diet every year to lose the extra holiday weight or simply start following healthy habits. However, some fat diet plans are often a bit overwhelming. For example, it requires a tremendous amount of self-discipline to drink only juices. Moreover, even after finishing a grueling detox diet plan, you might just go back to eating foods that are bad for you because of those days of deprivation. New studies issued in the *Medicine & Science in Sports & Exercise* shows that low-calorie diets may result in binge eating, which is not the right method for lasting weight loss.

Another research conducted by the researchers at Loughborough University showed that healthy, college-aged women who followed a calorie-restricted diet consumed an extra three hundred calories at dinner as compared to the control group who consumed three standard meals. They revealed that it was because they had lower levels of peptide YY (represses appetite) and higher levels of ghrelin (makes you hungry). They are most likely to go hog wild when you are feeling ravenous, and it's finally time to eat (Nawal Alajmi K. D.-O., 2016).

Another research published in *Cognitive Neuroscience* studied the brains of chronic dieters. They revealed that there was a weaker connection between the two regions of the brain in people who had a higher percentage of body fat. They showed that they might have an increased risk of getting obese because it's harder for them to set their temptations aside (Pin-Hao Andy Chen, 2016).

A few other studies, however, also revealed that you could increase your self-control through practice. Self-control, similar to any other kind of strength, also requires time to develop. However, you can consider focusing on a diet plan that can help you "reset" instead of putting all your efforts into developing your self-control to get healthy.

A reset is considered as a new start – one that can get your metabolism and your liver in good shape. The liver is the biggest solid organ of your body, and it's mainly responsible for removing toxins that can harm your health and well-being by polluting your system. Toxins keep accumulating in your body all the time, and even though it's the liver's job to handle this, it can sometimes get behind schedule, which can result in inflammation. It causes a lot of strain on your metabolism and results in weight gain, particularly around the abdomen. The best method to alleviate this inflammation is to follow a metabolism rest diet and give your digestive system a vacation (Olivia M. Farr, 2015).

Chapter 3: Recipes for Smoothies and Salads

If you want to lose weight and you have a particular period within which you want to achieve it, then here are some recipes that are going to be helpful.

Green Smoothie

Total Prep & Cooking Time: 2 minutes

Yields: 1 serving

Nutrition Facts: Calories: 144 | Carbs: 28.2g | Protein: 3.4g | Fat: 2.9g | Fiber: 4.8g

Ingredients:

- One cup each of
  - Almond milk
  - Raw spinach
- One-third of a cup of strawberries
- One orange, peeled

Method:

1. Add the peeled orange, strawberries, almond milk, and raw spinach in a blender and blend everything until you get a smooth paste. You can add extra water if required to achieve the desired thickness.

2. Pour out the smoothie into a glass and serve.

Strawberry Banana Smoothie

Total Prep & Cooking Time: 5 minutes

Yields: 2 servings

Nutrition Facts: Calories: 198| Carbs: 30.8g | Protein: 5.9g | Fat: 7.1g | Fiber: 4.8g

Ingredients:

- Half a cup each of
  - o Milk
  - o Greek yogurt
- One banana, frozen and quartered
- Two cups of fresh strawberries, halved

Method:

1. Add the milk, Greek yogurt, banana, and strawberries into a high-powered blender and blend until you get a smooth mixture.

2. Pour the smoothie equally into two separate glasses and serve.

Notes:

- *Don't add ice to the smoothie as it can make it watery very quickly. Using frozen bananas will keep your smoothie cold.*

- *As you're using bananas and strawberries, there is no need to add any artificial sweetener.*

Salmon Citrus Salad

Total Prep & Cooking Time: 20 minutes

Yields: 6 servings

Nutrition Facts: Calories: 336 | Carbs: 20g | Protein: 17g | Fat: 21g | Fiber: 5g

Ingredients:

- One pound of Citrus Salmon (slow-roasted)
- Half of an English cucumber, sliced
- One tomato (large), sliced into a quarter of an inch thick pieces
- One grapefruit, peeled and cut into segments
- Two oranges, peeled and cut into segments
- Three beets, roasted and quartered
- One avocado
- Boston lettuce leaves
- Two tablespoons of red wine vinegar
- Half of a red onion
- Flakey salt
- Aleppo pepper flakes

For the Citrus Shallot Vinaigrette,

- Five tablespoons of olive oil (extra-virgin)
- One clove of garlic, smashed
- Salt and pepper
- One and a half tablespoons of rice wine vinegar
- Two tablespoons of orange juice or fresh lemon juice
- One tablespoon of shallot, minced

Method:

For preparing the Citrus Shallot Vinaigrette:

1. Add the ingredients for the vinaigrette in a bowl and whisk them together.

2. Keep the mixture aside.

For assembling the salad,

1. Add the onions and vinegar in a small bowl and pickle them by letting them sit for about fifteen minutes.

2. In the meantime, place the lettuce leaves on the serving plate.

3. Dice the avocado in half and eliminate the pit. Then scoop the flesh and add them onto the plate. Sprinkle a dash of flakey salt and Aleppo pepper on top to season it.

4. Add the quartered beets onto the serving plate along with the grapefruit and orange segments.

5. Salt the cucumber and tomato slices lightly and add them onto the plate.

6. Then, scatter the pickled onions on top and cut the salmon into bits and add it on the plate.

7. Lastly, drizzle the Citrus Shallot Vinaigrette on top of the salad and finish off with a dash of flakey salt.

Chapter 4: Quick and Easy Breakfast and Main Course Recipes

Quinoa Salad
Total Prep & Cooking Time: 40 minutes

Yields: Eight servings

Nutrition Facts: Calories: 205 | Carbs: 25.9g | Protein: 6.1g | Fat: 9.4g | Fiber: 4.6g

Ingredients:

- One tablespoon of red wine vinegar
- One-fourth of a cup each of
    - Lemon juice (about two to three lemons)
    - Olive oil
- One cup each of
    - Quinoa (uncooked), rinsed with the help of a fine-mesh colander
    - Flat-leaf parsley (from a single large bunch), finely chopped
- Three-fourth of a cup of red onion (one small red onion), chopped
- One red bell pepper (medium-sized), chopped
- One cucumber (medium-sized), seeded and chopped
- One and a half cups of chickpeas (cooked), or One can of chickpeas (about fifteen ounces), rinsed and drained
- Two cloves of garlic, minced or pressed
- Two cups of water
- Black pepper, freshly ground
- Half a teaspoon of fine sea salt

Method:

1. Place a medium-sized saucepan over medium-high heat and add the rinsed quinoa into it along with the water. Allow the mixture to boil and then reduce the heat and simmer it. Cook for about fifteen minutes so that the quinoa has absorbed all the water. As time goes on, decrease the heat and maintain a gentle simmer. Take the saucepan away from the heat and cover it with a lid. Allow the cooked quinoa to rest for about five minutes to give it some time to increase in size.

2. Add the onions, bell pepper, cucumber, chickpeas, and parsley in a large serving bowl and mix them together. Keep the mixture aside.

3. Add the garlic, vinegar, lemon juice, olive oil, and salt in another small bowl and whisk the ingredients so that they are appropriately combined. Keep this mixture aside.

4. When the cooked quinoa has almost cooled down, transfer it to the serving bowl. Add the dressing on top and toss to combine everything together.

5. Add an extra pinch of sea salt and the black pepper to season according to your preference. Allow the salad to rest for five to ten minutes before serving it for the best results.

6. You can keep the salad in the refrigerator for up to four days. Make sure to cover it properly.

7. You can serve it at room temperature or chilled.

Notes: Instead of cooking additional quinoa, you can use about three cups of leftover quinoa for making this salad. Moreover, you can also serve this salad with fresh greens and an additional drizzle of lemon juice and olive oil. You can also add a dollop of cashew sour cream or crumbled feta cheese as a topping.

Herb and Goat Cheese Omelet

Total Prep & Cooking Time: 20 minutes

Yields: Two servings

Nutrition Facts: Calories: 233 | Carbs: 3.6g | Protein: 16g | Fat: 17.6g | Fiber: 1g

Ingredients:

- Half a cup each of
  - Red bell peppers (3 x quarter-inch), julienne-cut
  - Zucchini, thinly sliced
- Four large eggs
- Two teaspoons of olive oil, divided
- One-fourth of a cup of goat cheese (one ounce), crumbled
- Half a teaspoon of fresh tarragon, chopped
- One teaspoon each of
  - Fresh parsley, chopped
  - Fresh chives, chopped
- One-eighth of a teaspoon of salt
- One-fourth of a teaspoon of black pepper, freshly ground (divided)
- One tablespoon of water

Method:

1. Break the eggs into a bowl and add one tablespoon of water into it. Whisk them together and add in one-eighth of a teaspoon each of salt and ground black pepper.

2. In another small bowl, mix the goat cheese, tarragon, and parsley and keep it aside.

3. Place a nonstick skillet over medium heat and heat one teaspoon of olive oil in it. Add in the sliced zucchini, bell pepper, and the remaining one-eighth of a teaspoon of black pepper along with a dash of salt. Cook for about four minutes so that the bell pepper and zucchini get soft. Transfer the zucchini-bell pepper mixture onto a plate and cover it with a lid to keep it warm.

4. Add about half a teaspoon of oil into a skillet and add in half of the whisked egg into it. Do not stir the eggs and let the egg set slightly. Loosen the set edges of the omelet carefully with the help of a spatula. Tilt the skillet to move the uncooked part of the egg to the side. Keep following this method for about five seconds so that there is no more runny egg in the skillet. Add half of the crumbled goat cheese mixture evenly over the omelet and let it cook for another minute so that it sets.

5. Transfer the omelet onto a plate and fold it into thirds.

6. Repeat the process with the rest of the egg mixture, half a teaspoon of olive oil, and the goat cheese mixture.

7. Add the chopped chives on top of the omelets and serve with the bell pepper and zucchini mixture.

Mediterranean Cod

Total Prep & Cooking Time: 15 minutes

Yields: 4 servings

Nutrition Facts: Calories: 320 | Carbs: 31g | Protein: 35g | Fat: 8g | Fiber: 8g

Ingredients:

- One pound of spinach
- Four fillets of cod (almost one and a half pounds)
- Two zucchinis (medium-sized), chopped
- One cup of marinara sauce
- One-fourth of a teaspoon of red pepper, crushed
- Two cloves of garlic, chopped
- One tablespoon of olive oil
- Salt and pepper, according to taste
- Whole wheat roll, for serving

Method:

1. Place a ten-inch skillet on medium heat and add the marinara sauce and zucchini into it. Combine them together and let it simmer on medium heat.

2. Add the fillets of cod into the simmering sauce. Add one-fourth of a teaspoon each of salt and pepper too. Cover the skillet with a lid and let it cook for about seven minutes so that the cod gets just opaque throughout.

3. In the meantime, place a five-quart saucepot on medium heat and heat the olive oil in it. Add in the crushed red pepper and minced garlic. Stir and cook for about a minute.

4. Then, add in the spinach along with one-eighth of a teaspoon of salt. Cover the saucepot with a lid and let it cook for about five minutes, occasionally stirring so that the spinach gets wilted.

5. Add the spinach on the plates and top with the sauce and cod mixture and serve with the whole wheat roll.

Grilled Chicken and Veggies

Total Prep & Cooking Time: 35 minutes

Yields: 4 servings

Nutrition Facts: Calories: 305 | Carbs: 11g | Protein: 26g | Fat: 17g | Fiber: 3g

Ingredients:

For the marinade,

- Four cloves of garlic, crushed

- One-fourth of a cup each of
  - Fresh lemon juice
  - Olive oil
- One teaspoon each of
  - Salt
  - Smoked paprika
  - Dried oregano
- Black pepper, according to taste
- Half a teaspoon of red chili flakes

For the grilling,

- Two to three zucchinis or courgette (large), cut into thin slices
- Twelve to sixteen spears of asparagus, woody sides trimmed
- Broccoli
- Two bell peppers, seeds eliminated and cut into thin slices
- Four pieces of chicken breasts (large), skinless and de-boned

Method:

1. Preheat your griddle or grill pan.

2. Sprinkle some salt on top of the chicken breasts to season them. Keep them aside to rest while you prepare the marinade.

3. For the marinade, mix all the ingredients properly.

4. Add about half of the marinade over the vegetables and the other half over the seasoned chicken breasts. Allow the marinade to rest for a couple of minutes.

5. Place the chicken pieces on the preheated grill. Grill for about five to seven minutes on each side until they are cooked according to your preference. The time on the grill depends on the thickness of the chicken breasts.

6. Remove them from the grill and cover them using a foil. Set it aside to rest and prepare to grill the vegetables in the meantime.

7. Grill the vegetables for a few minutes until they begin to char and are crispy yet tender.

8. Remove them from the grill and transfer them onto a serving plate. Serve the veggies along with the grilled chicken and add the lemon wedges on the side for squeezing.

Notes: You can add as much or as little vegetables as you like. The vegetable amounts are given only as a guide. Moreover, feel free to replace some of them with the vegetables you like to eat.

Stuffed Peppers

Total Prep & Cooking Time: 50 minutes

Yields: 4 servings

Nutrition Facts: Calories: 438 | Carbs: 32g | Protein: 32g | Fat: 20g | Fiber: 5g

Ingredients:

For the stuffed peppers,

- One pound of ground chicken or turkey
- Four bell peppers (large) of any color
- One and a quarter of a cups of cheese, shredded
- One and a half cups of brown rice, cooked (you can use cauliflower rice or quinoa)
- One can (about fourteen ounces) of fire-roasted diced tomatoes along with its juices
- Two teaspoons of olive oil (extra-virgin)
- One teaspoon each of
  o Garlic powder
  o Ground cumin
- One tablespoon of ground chili powder
- One-fourth of a teaspoon of black pepper
- Half a teaspoon of kosher salt

For serving,

- Sour cream or Greek yogurt

- Salsa

- Freshly chopped cilantro

- Avocado, sliced

- Freshly squeezed lemon juice

Method:

1. Preheat your oven to 375 degrees Fahrenheit.

2. Take a nine by thirteen-inch baking dish and coat it lightly with a nonstick cooking spray.

3. Take the bell peppers and slice them from top to bottom into halves. Remove the membranes and the seeds. Keep the bell peppers in the baking dish with the cut-side facing upwards.

4. Place a large, nonstick skillet on medium-high heat and heat the olive oil in it. Add in the chicken, pepper, salt, garlic powder, ground cumin, and chili powder and cook for about four minutes so that the chicken is cooked through and gets brown. Break apart the chicken while it's cooking. Drain off any excess liquid and then add in the can of diced tomatoes along with the juices. Allow it to simmer for a minute.

5. Take the pan away from the heat. Add in the cooked rice along with three-fourth of a cup of the shredded cheese and stir everything together.

6. Add this filling inside the peppers and add the remaining shredded cheese as a topping.

7. Add a little amount of water into the pan containing the peppers so that it barely covers the bottom of the pan.

8. Keep it uncovered and bake it in the oven for twenty-five to thirty-five minutes so that the cheese gets melted and the peppers get soft.

9. Add any of your favorite fixings as a topping and serve hot.

Notes:

- *For preparing the stuffed peppers ahead of time, make sure to allow the rice and chicken mixture to cool down completely before filling the peppers. You can prepare the stuffed peppers before time, and then you have to cover it with a lid and keep it in the refrigerator for a maximum of twenty-four hours before baking the peppers.*

- *If you're planning to reheat the stuffed peppers, gently reheat them in your oven or microwave. If you're using a microwave for this purpose, make sure to cut the peppers into pieces to warm them evenly.*

- *You can store any leftovers in the freezer for up to three months. Alternatively, you can keep them in the refrigerator for up to four days. Allow it to thaw in the fridge overnight.*

Brussels Sprouts With Honey Mustard Chicken

Total Prep & Cooking Time: Fifty minutes

Yields: Four servings

Nutrition Facts: Calories: 360 | Carbs: 14.5g | Protein: 30.8g | Fat: 20g | Fiber: 3.7g

Ingredients:

- One and a half pounds of Brussels sprouts, divided into two halves
- Two pounds of chicken thighs, skin-on and bone-in (about four medium-sized thighs)
- Three cloves of garlic, minced
- One-fourth of a large onion, cut into slices
- One tablespoon each of
  - Honey
  - Whole-grain mustard
  - Dijon mustard
- Two tablespoons of freshly squeezed lemon juice (one lemon)
- One-fourth of a cup plus two tablespoons of olive oil (extra-virgin)
- Freshly ground black pepper
- Kosher salt
- Non-stick cooking spray

Method:

1. Preheat your oven to 425 degrees Fahrenheit.

2. Take a large baking sheet and grease it with nonstick cooking spray. Keep it aside.

3. Add the minced garlic, honey, whole-grain mustard, Dijon mustard, one tablespoon of the lemon juice, one-fourth cup of the olive oil in a medium-sized bowl and mix them together. Add the Kosher salt and black pepper to season according to your preference.

4. Dip the chicken thighs into the sauce with the help of tongs and coat both sides. Transfer the things on the baking sheet. You can get rid of any extra sauce.

5. Mix the red onion and Brussels sprouts in a medium-sized bowl and drizzle one tablespoon of lemon juice along with the remaining two tablespoons of olive oil onto it. Toss everything together until the vegetables are adequately coated.

6. Place the red onion-Brussels sprouts mixture on the baking sheet around the chicken pieces. Ensure that the chicken and vegetables are not overlapping.

7. Sprinkle a little amount of salt and pepper on the top and keep it in the oven to roast for about thirty to thirty-five minutes so that the Brussels sprouts get crispy and the chicken has an internal temperature of 165 degrees Fahrenheit and has turned golden brown.

8. Serve hot.

Quinoa Stuffed Chicken

Total Prep & Cooking Time: 50 minutes

Yields: Four servings

Nutrition Facts: Calories: 355 | Carbs: 28g | Protein: 30g | Fat: 13g | Fiber: 4g

Ingredients:

- One and a half cups of chicken broth
- Three-fourths of a cup of quinoa (any color of your choice)
- Four chicken breasts (boneless and skinless)
- One lime, zested and one tablespoon of lime juice
- One-fourth of a cup of cilantro, chipped
- One-third of a cup of unsweetened coconut, shaved or coconut chips
- One Serrano pepper, seeded and diced
- Two cloves of garlic, minced
- Half a cup of red onion, diced
- Three-fourth of a cup of bell pepper, diced
- One tablespoon of coconut oil
- One teaspoon each of
  - Salt
  - Chili powder
  - Ground cumin

Method:

1. Preheat your oven to 375 degrees Fahrenheit.

2. Take a rimmed baking sheet and line it with parchment paper.

3. Place a medium-sized saucepan over medium-high heat and add the coconut oil in it. After it has melted, add in the Serrano peppers, garlic, red onion, and bell pepper and sauté for about one to two minutes so

that they soften just a bit. Make sure that the vegetables are still bright in color. Then transfer the cooked vegetables into a bowl.

4. Add the quinoa in the empty sauce pot and increase the heat to high. Pour the chicken broth in it along with half a teaspoon of salt. Close the lid of the pot and bring it to a boil, allowing the quinoa to cook for about fifteen minutes so that the surface of the quinoa develops vent holes, and the broth has absorbed completely. Take the pot away from the heat and allow it to steam for an additional five minutes.

5. In the meantime, cut a slit along the long side in each chicken breast. It will be easier with the help of a boning knife. You are making a deep pocket in each breast, having a half-inch border around the remaining three attached sides. Keep the knife parallel to the cutting board and cut through the middle of the breast and leaving the opposite side attached. Try to cut it evenly as it's challenging to cook thick uncut portions properly in the oven. After that, add salt, cumin, and chili powder on all sides of the chicken.

6. When the quinoa has turned fluffy, add in the lime juice, lime zest, shaved coconut, and sautéed vegetables and stir them in. Taste the mixture and adjust the salt as per your preference.

7. Add the confetti quinoa mixture inside the cavity of the chicken breast. Place the stuffed breasts on the baking sheet with the quinoa facing upwards. They'll look like open envelopes.

8. Bake them in the oven for about twenty minutes.

9. Serve warm.

Kale and Sweet Potato Frittata

Total Prep & Cooking Time: 30 minutes

Yields: 4 servings

Nutrition Facts: Calories: 144 | Carbs: 10g | Protein: 7g | Fat: 9g | Fiber: 2g

Ingredients:

- Three ounces of goat cheese
- Two cloves of garlic
- Half of a red onion (small)
- Two cups each of
    - Sweet potatoes
    - Firmly packed kale, chopped
- Two tablespoons of olive oil
- One cup of half-and-half
- Six large eggs
- Half a teaspoon of pepper, freshly ground
- One teaspoon of Kosher salt

Method:

1. Preheat your oven to 350 degrees Fahrenheit.

2. Add the eggs, half-and-half, salt, and black pepper in a bowl and whisk everything together.

3. Place a ten-inch ovenproof nonstick skillet over medium heat and add one tablespoon of oil in it. Sauté the sweet potatoes in the skillet for about eight to ten minutes so that they turn soft and golden brown. Transfer them onto a plate and keep warm.

4. Next, add in the remaining one tablespoon of oil and sauté the kale along with the red onions and garlic in it for about three to four minutes so that the kale gets soft and wilted. Then, add in the whisked egg mixture evenly over the vegetables and cook for an additional three minutes.

5. Add some goat cheese on the top and bake it in the oven for ten to fourteen minutes so that it sets.

Walnut, Ginger, and Pineapple Oatmeal

Total Prep & Cooking Time: 30 minutes

Yields: 4 servings

Nutrition Facts: Calories: 323 | Carbs: 61g | Protein: 6g | Fat: 8g | Fiber: 5g

Ingredients:

- Two large eggs
- Two cups each of
  - Fresh pineapple, coarsely chopped
  - Old-fashioned rolled oats
  - Whole milk
- One cup of walnuts, chopped
- Half a cup of maple syrup
- One piece of ginger
- Two teaspoons of vanilla extract
- Half a teaspoon of salt

Method:

1. Preheat your oven to 400 degrees Fahrenheit.

2. Add the ginger, walnuts, pineapple, oats, and salt in a large bowl and mix them together. Add the mixture evenly among four ten-ounce ramekins and keep them aside.

3. Whisk the eggs along with the milk, maple syrup, and vanilla extract in a medium-sized bowl. Pour one-quarter of this mixture into each ramekin containing the oat-pineapple mixture.

4. Keep the ramekins on the baking sheet and bake them in the oven for about twenty-five minutes until the oats turn light golden brown on the top and have set properly.

5. Serve with some additional maple syrup on the side.

Caprese Salad

Total Prep & Cooking Time: 15 minutes

Yields: 4 servings

Nutrition Facts: Calories: 216 | Carbs: 4g | Protein: 13g | Fat: 16g | Fiber: 1g

Ingredients:

For the salad,

- Nine basil leaves (medium-sized)
- Eight ounces of fresh whole-milk mozzarella cheese
- Two tomatoes (medium-sized)
- One-fourth of a teaspoon of black pepper, freshly ground
- Half a teaspoon of Kosher salt, or one-fourth of a teaspoon of sea salt

For the dressing,

- One teaspoon of Dijon mustard
- One tablespoon each of
  - o Balsamic vinegar
  - o Olive oil

Method:

1. Add the olive oil, balsamic vinegar, and Dijon mustard into a small bowl and whisk them together with the help of a small hand whisk so that you get a smooth salad dressing. Keep it aside.

2. Cut the tomatoes into thin slices and try to get ten slices in total.

3. Cut the mozzarella into nine thin slices with the help of a sharp knife.

4. Place the slices of tomatoes and mozzarella on a serving plate, alternating and overlapping one another. Then, add the basil leaves on the top.

5. Season the salad with black pepper and salt and drizzle the prepared dressing on top.

6. Serve immediately.

One-Pot Chicken Soup

Total Prep & Cooking Time: 30 minutes

Yields: 6 servings

Nutrition Facts: Calories: 201 | Carbs: 20g | Protein: 16g | Fat: 7g | Fiber: 16g

Ingredients:

- Three cups of loosely packed chopped kale (or other greens of your choice)
- Two cups of chicken, shredded
- One can of white beans (about fifteen ounces), slightly drained
- Eight cups of broth (vegetable broth or chicken broth)
- Four cloves of garlic, minced
- One cup of yellow or white onion, diced
- One tablespoon of avocado oil (skip if you are using bacon)
- One strip of uncured bacon, chopped (optional)
- Black pepper + sea salt, according to taste

Method:

1. Place a Dutch oven or a large pot over medium heat. When it gets hot, add in the oil or bacon (optional), stirring occasionally, and allow it to get hot for about a minute.

2. Then, add in the diced onion and sauté for four to five minutes, occasionally stirring so that the onions get fragrant and translucent. Add in the minced garlic next and sauté for another two to three minutes. Be careful so as not to burn the ingredients.

3. Then, add the chicken, slightly drained white beans, and broth and bring the mixture to a simmer. Cook for about ten minutes to bring out all the flavors. Taste the mixture and add salt and pepper to season according to your preference. Add in the chopped kale in the last few minutes of cooking. Cover the pot and let it cook until the kale has wilted.

4. Serve hot.

Notes: You can store any leftovers in the freezer for up to a month. Or, you can store them in the refrigerator for a maximum of three to four days. Simply reheat on the stovetop or in the microwave and eat it later.

Chocolate Pomegranate Truffles

Total Prep & Cooking Time: 10 minutes

Yields: Twelve to Fourteen truffles

Nutrition Facts: Calories: 95 | Carbs: 26g | Protein: 1g | Fat: 2g | Fiber: 3g

Ingredients:

- One-third of a cup of pomegranate arils
- Half a teaspoon each of
  - Vanilla extract
  - Ground cinnamon
- Half a cup of ground flax seed
- Two tablespoons of cocoa powder (unsweetened)
- About one tablespoon of water
- One and a half cups of pitted Medjool dates
- One-eighth of a teaspoon of salt

Method:

1. Add the pitted dates in a food processor and blend until it begins to form a ball. Add some water and pulse again. Add in the vanilla, cinnamon, flax seeds, cocoa powder, and salt and blend until everything is combined properly.

2. Turn off the food processor and unplug it. Add in the pomegranate arils and fold them in the mixture so that they are distributed evenly.

3. Make twelve to fourteen balls using the mixture. You can create an outer coating or topping if you want by rolling the balls in finely shredded coconut or cocoa powder.

Notes: You can store the chocolate pomegranate truffles in the fridge in an air-tight container for a maximum of three days.

CPSIA information can be obtained
at www.ICGtesting.com
Printed in the USA
LVHW080104191021
700772LV00009B/330

9 781913 710491